D1104288

Fact

of the

Day 1

Fact

First Edition

of the

Day 1

250 FACTS FOR THE CURIOUS

DANNY SHERIDAN

Danny Sheridan
Fact of the Day 1 (1st Edition)
danny@factoftheday1.com

First Printing: December 2020
ISBN-13 979-8-59070-642-6

This book is dedicated to the team at Code.org for changing the world through expanding access to computer science education for students across the globe. The internet is increasingly foundational for every career, civic participation, and accessing humanity's shared knowledge.

"Never doubt that a small group of thoughtful, committed citizens can change the world. Indeed, it is the only thing that ever has."

— MARGARET MEAD

About Code.org

Code.org is a nonprofit dedicated to expanding access to computer science in schools and increasing participation by young women and students from other underrepresented groups. Their vision is that every student in every school has the opportunity to learn computer science as part of their core K-12 education. Code.org also created the annual Hour of Code campaign, which has engaged more than 15% of all students in the world.

About the Author

Danny Sheridan's entrepreneurial journey started in Cleveland, Ohio. The company he founded in high school, Woodside Distributors, sold products online predominantly through the Amazon Marketplace. Since his teenage years, he has been fascinated by Amazon's péculiar and innovative culture. Upon graduation from the Ross School of Business at the University of Michigan, Danny joined Amazon as a Product Manager.

With the goal of sharing trends in tech, business, and entrepreneurship, he started writing a daily fact on a whiteboard. Sending a photo to friends, family, and colleagues each day quickly became so cumbersome that he turned it into an email list, and *Fact of the Day 1* was born. In the two years since its inception, *Fact of the Day 1* has delivered data-driven facts that, in the words of readers, "tickle the brain" and "are bite-sized yet useful." Attracting over 50,000 readers, facts now prompt water cooler discussions around the world and can be heard during team meeting 'icebreakers' from fulfillment centers to corporate office conference rooms. Danny lives in Seattle, where he bounces around different neighborhoods every year with his goldendoodle Markley.

Opinions expressed are solely my own and do not express the views or opinions of Code.org or my employer.

Table of Contents

SECTION 1

ARE RIGHT, A LOT

CHAPTER 1

AMAZON ORIGIN STORIES

Source: **Marketplace.org**
Published: July 2019

Amazon's logo through the years

As our customers' expectations of Amazon change, so does the logo.

1995 to 1997: Amazon River

amazon.com

1997 to 1998: Earth's biggest bookstore

amazon.com
EARTH'S BIGGEST BOOKSTORE

1998: The circle with capital letters

AMAZ◯N.CoM

1998 to 2000: Orange curve

amazon.com

2000 to 2012: a-to-z smile

amazon.com

2012 to present day: drop the ".com"

amazon

Source: Marketplace.org
Published: July 2019

Amazon's Logo Through the Years

As our customers' expectations of Amazon change, so does the logo.

1995 to 1997:

1997 to 1998:

1998:

1998 to 2000:

2000 to present day:

Images: https://logos.fandom.com/wiki/Amazon

Source: Internet Association October 20, 2020
Published: May 2017

Amazon's Early Investors

"Amazon started as a very small company. I was driving all of the packages to the post office myself in my 1987 Chevy Blazer.

When I raised money for Amazon, I had to raise $1 million. Investors each put in $50k and [collectively] received 20% of the company.

40 people told me no. The first question was always, "what is the internet?" so I had to start by walking through that; this was early 1995."

-Jeff Bezos

Source: Internet Association

Published: May 2017

Amazon's Early Investors

"Amazon started as a very small company. I was driving all of the packages to the post office myself in my 1987 Chevy Blazer.

When I raised money for Amazon, I had to raise $1 million. Investors each put in $50k and [collectively] received 20% of the company.

40 people told me no. The first question was always, *"what is the internet?"* so I had to start by walking through that; this was early 1995."

—Jeff Bezos

Source: Wall Street Journal

Published: October 2011

Amazon's first beta test

At launch, the Amazon.com site wasn't even truly finished. The philosophy was to get to market quickly and to fix problems and improve the site as people started using it.

The first beta test for Amazon.com was performed in April 1995.

Among the bugs discovered is that it's possible to order a negative quantity of books; the system would try to credit the customers' card!

Jonathan Leblang, who later joined Amazon as an employee in 1999, discovered this bug.

Source: Wall Street Journal

Published: October 2011

Amazon's First Beta Test

"At launch, the Amazon.com site wasn't even truly finished. The philosophy was to get to market quickly and to fix problems and improve the site as people started using it.

The first beta test for Amazon.com was performed in April 1995. Among the bugs discovered is that it's possible to order a negative quantity of books; the system would try to credit the customers' card!"

-Jonathan Leblang

discovered and reported the bug in 1995. Leblang joined as an Amazonian four years later, and today he works as a Director of Product at Amazon.

Source: Amazon Press Release
Published: September 1997

Electronic Commerce Catapults with Powerful New Features

"Amazon offers customers these new features that are not available anywhere online or in physical stores. We are making Amazon.com the easiest, most enjoyable, and most effective way for customers to find their next book."
—Jeff Bezos

Features Launched

1. Recommended Center:
   personalized suggestions to choose your next book.

2. Subject-browsing areas:
   such as fiction, mystery, romance, bestsellers, and award winning.

3. 1-Click Ordering:
   proprietary software that gives customers the ability to make purchases on the web with just one click of the mouse.

Source: Amazon Press Release
Published: September 1997

Electronic Commerce Catapults with Powerful New Features

"Amazon offers customers these new features that are not available anywhere online or in physical stores. We are making Amazon.com the easiest, most enjoyable, and most effective way for customers to find their next book."

-Jeff Bezos

Features launched:

1. Recommendation center: personalized suggestions to choose your next book.
2. Subject-browsing areas: such as fiction, mystery, romance, bestsellers, and award winning.
3. 1-Click Ordering: Proprietary software that gives customers the ability to make purchases on the Web with just one click of the mouse, eliminating the need for customers to fill out order information every time they return to the site.

Source: Greg Linden
Published: April 2006

Recommended for You

Around 1998, a software engineer at Amazon.com, Greg Linden, asked himself, "What if Amazon recommended impulse buys at checkout, based upon the products in the customer's shopping cart?"

Grocery stores had been offering candy bars and AA batteries in their checkout lanes for decades.

So, Linden hacked up a prototype and started showing it to his team. A Senior Vice President of Marketing saw it and didn't like it for the fear that it distracts shoppers from checking out.

Greg decided to A/B test it anyway and measure incremental sales.

The results were clear.

Having recommendations won by a wide margin. With urgency, shopping cart recommendations launched.

"In my experience, innovation can only come from the bottom. Those closest to the problem are in the best position to solve it."

— Greg Linden

Source: Greg Linden
Published: April 2006

Recommended for You

Around 1998, a software engineer at Amazon.com, Greg Linden, asked himself, *"What if Amazon recommended impulse buys at checkout, based upon the products in the customer's shopping cart?"* Grocery stores had been proffering candy bars and AA batteries in their checkout lanes for decades.

So, he hacked up a prototype and started showing it to his team. A Senior Vice President of Marketing saw it and didn't like it for the fear that it distracts shoppers from checking out. Greg decided to A/B test it anyway and measure incremental sales. The results were clear. Having recommendations won by a wide margin. With urgency, shopping cart recommendations launched.

"In my experience, innovation can only come from the bottom. Those closest to the problem are in the best position to solve it."

— **Greg Linden**

Amazon.com shopping cart recommendations. The recommendations are based on the items in the customer's cart. Image: IEEE Internet Computing.

Source: Washington Post   February 12, 2020
Published: August 2013

Just Do It Award

In February 1998, the Amazon Customer Service queues were backed up with inquiries. An associate came up with a solution: Whoever could close out 250 inquiries in 24 hours would receive an extra $200.

All the queues were cleared. When Jeff Bezos heard, he thought about what made her efforts so great and identified four points:

1) She had undertaken the effort on her own initiative. She wasn't asked to come up with a solution to the problem.

2) She didn't ask permission, which would have slowed down the process.

3) Her idea was well thought out.

4) Her idea was a success. °° This is the least important.

Since then, the "Just Do It" Award has rewarded Amazon employees around the world for taking the effort to get things done on behalf of Customers.

Source: Washington Post
Published: August 2013

Just Do It Award

In February 1998, the Amazon Customer Service queues were backed up with inquiries. An associate came up with a solution: whoever could close out 250 inquiries in 24 hours would receive an extra *$200*. All the queues were cleared. When Jeff Bezos heard, he thought about what made her efforts so great and identified four points:

1. She had undertaken the effort on her own initiative. She wasn't asked to come up with a solution to the problem.
2. She didn't ask permission, which would have slowed down the process.
3. Her idea was well thought out.
4. Her idea was a success. (This is the least important.)

Since then, the "*Just Do It*" Award has rewarded Amazon employees around the world for taking the effort to get things done on behalf of Customers.

Source: The Loop Insight
Published: August 2013

The Lichen Loophole

In the first few years of Amazon — 1994 to 1997 — the team had to buy products from wholesalers who wouldn't just sell one or two books — they had a 10 book minimum.

"I tried to negotiate with them and said, let us just pay a small fee, and you waive the 10 book minimum. They wouldn't go for it." - Jeff Bezos

So Amazon figured out a loophole. It turned out that you just had to place an order for 10 books; you didn't actually have to get 10 books.

"We found an obscure book on lichens that none of our wholesalers actually carried." - Jeff Bezos

Lichen: a composite organism consisting of fungus and alga

Source: The Loop Insight
Published: August 2013

The Lichen Loophole

In the first few years of Amazon — *1994 to 1997* — the team had to buy products from wholesalers who wouldn't sell just one or two books — they had a ten-book minimum, and that was non-negotiable.

"The problem was, the wholesalers had 10-book minimum orders. I tried to negotiate with them and said, "Let us just pay a small fee, and you waive the 10-book order," and so on. But they wouldn't go for it. So we figured out a loophole. It turned out that you just had to place an order for 10 books; you didn't actually have to get 10 books. We found an obscure book on lichens that none of our wholesalers actually carried."

— **Jeff Bezos**

Lichen: a simple slow-growing plant that typically forms a low crusty, leaflike, or branching growth on rocks, walls, and trees.

Source: Amazon Press Release
Published: June 1999

They'd have locked us up as dangerous

In October 1997 Amazon.com became the first internet retailer to serve 1 million customers, and its cumulative customer base grew tenfold in 21 months — equivalent to the population of Greece.

"If anyone had predicted in 1995 that we'd have 10 million Amazonians by now, they'd be locked up as dangerous.

We certainly didn't expect it, and we're extremely grateful. We're celebrating — but quickly — and taking this opportunity to re-commit ourselves to our customers."

-Jeff Bezos

Source: Amazon Press Release
Published: June 1999

They'd Have Locked Us Up As Dangerous

In October 1997, Amazon.com became the first Internet retailer to serve *1 million customers*, and its cumulative customer base has grown tenfold in *21 months* — equivalent to the population of Greece.

"If anyone had predicted in 1995 that we'd have 10 million Amazonians by now, they'd have been locked up as dangerous. We certainly didn't expect it, and we're extremely grateful. We're celebrating — but quickly — and taking this opportunity to re-commit ourselves to our customers."

—Jeff Bezos

Source: Jonathan Leblang   March 3, 2020
Published: February 2020

Amazon holiday gifts to customers

In 1996 Amazon sent every single customer a gift. Customers would open the package to find a mouse pad with a quote from Groucho Marx (the popular American comedian): Outside of a dog, a book is man's best friend. Inside of a dog, it's too dark to read.

From 1997 to 2000, Amazon sent top customers and employees a holiday gift of an insulated coffee mug. The mugs were adorned with quotes about books and reading.

The team reserved mugs so that if a customer contacted Customer Service asking why they didn't get a mug, they could be sent one.

Attached are photos of the gifts and the associated letters from Jeff Bezos.

Source: Jonathan Leblang
Published: February 2020

Amazon Holiday Gifts to Customers

In 1996 Amazon sent every single customer a gift. Customers (like Richard who tweeted about it in March 2019) would open the box to find a mouse pad with a quote from Groucho Marx (the popular American comedian), *"Outside of a dog, a book is man's best friend. Inside of a dog, it's too dark to read."*

From 1997 to 2000, Amazon sent top customers and employees a holiday gift of an insulated coffee travel mug. The mugs were adorned with quotes about books and reading. The team reserved mugs so that if a customer contacted Customer Service asking why they didn't get a mug, they could be sent one.

Gifts (mugs and a mouse pad) that were gifts from Amazon to customers from 1997 to 2000. Included with each gift was a thank you note signed by Jeff Bezos. Images: Phil Vandecar (coffee mugs) and Jonathan Leblang (mouse pad).

Source: Amazon Press Releases   October 16
Published: 1995 to 2001

Early Amazon Categories

Category	Launch Date	Customers
Books	July 1995	undisclosed
Music	June 1998	undisclosed
DVD and Video	November 1998	"millions"
Auction	March 1999	8 million
z Shops	September 1999	12 million
Video Games	November 1999	13 million
Gift Ideas	November 1999	13 million
Software	November 1999	13 million
Home Improvement	November 1999	13 million
Lawn and Patio	April 2000	17 million
Health and Beauty	April 2000	17 million
Kitchen	May 2000	20 million
Computers	September 2000	undisclosed
Camera and Photo	October 2000	23 million
Baby	May 2001	32 million

Source: Amazon Press Releases
Published: 1995 to 2001

Early Amazon Categories

Books first. Music and video next. Here are the categories available on Amazon.com, ordered by the launch date.

Category	Launch Date	# of Amazon Customers
Books	July 1995	Undisclosed
Music	June 1998	Undisclosed
DVD & Video	November 1998	"millions"
Auction	March 1999	8 million
zShops	September 1999	12 million
Video Games	November 1999	13 million
Gift Ideas	November 1999	13 million
Software	November 1999	13 million
Home Improvement	November 1999	13 million
Lawn and Patio	April 2000	17 million
Health & Beauty	April 2000	17 million
Kitchen	May 2000	20 million
Computers	September 2000	Undisclosed
Camera and Photo	October 2000	23 million
Baby	May 2001	32 million

Source: Harvard Business Review

Published: October 2007

March 17, 2020

"You're going to let anybody take Amazon traffic?"

This episode is one of the highlights of our corporate history — one that speaks to persistence and relentlesness.

Background: Amazon gets selection on our website by inviting third-party sellers to participate on the website alongside us.

Experiments: We launched Auctions (March 1999) but we didn't like the results. Next we created zShops which was fixed-price selling where each offer has its own detail page (September 1999). We still didn't like the results.

Solution: If Amazon is offering a product and you're a third-party seller with the product to sell, you can go on our own detail page, and underbid us.

Internal tension: It was a very controversial decision internally at the time. Our retail buyers objected:
" Let me just make sure I understand this. I might get stuck with 10,000 units of a camera because you're going to let anybody come in and take Amazon traffic?" Leadership said, "Yeah, we are."

Outcome: When we went to the single-detail-page model, our third-party business really took off. When the internal conversation gets too hard, we take a simpleminded approach. We convert it into a straightforward problem by saying, " Well, what's better for the consumer?"

Source: Harvard Business Review
Published: October 2007

You're going to let anybody take Amazon traffic?

"This episode is one of the highlights of our corporate history—one that speaks to persistence and relentlessness."

— **Jeff Bezos**

Background: Amazon gets selection on our website by inviting third-party sellers to participate on the website alongside us.

Experiments: We launched Auctions (March 1999), but we didn't like the results. Next we created zShops which was fixed-price selling where each offer has its own detail page (September 1999). We still didn't like the results.

Solution: If Amazon is offering a product and you're a third-party seller with the product to sell, you can go on our own detail page, and underbid us.

Internal tension: It was a very controversial decision internally at the time. Our retail buyers objected: "Let me just make sure I understand this. I might get stuck with 10,000 units of a camera because you're going to let anybody come in and take Amazon traffic?" Leadership said, "Yeah, we are."

Outcome: When we went to the single-detail-page model, our third-party business really took off. When the internal conversation gets too hard, we take a simpleminded approach. We convert it into a straightforward problem by saying, "Well, what's better for the consumer?"

Source: 2002 Letter to Shareholders   June 7
Published: 2003

Why Amazon.com is peculiar

"In many ways, Amazon.com is not a normal store:

- We turn our inventory 19 times a year.
- We personalize the store for each and every customer
- We trade real estate for technology (which gets cheaper and more capable every year)
- We display customer reviews critical of our products
- You can make a purchase with a few seconds and one click
- We put used products next to new ones so you can choose
- We share our prime real estate - our product detail pages - with third parties, and, if they can offer better value, we let them. "

— Jeff Bezos

Source: 2002 Letter to Shareholders
Published: April 2003

Why Amazon.com is Peculiar

In many ways, Amazon.com is not a normal store:

- We turn our inventory *19* times in a year.
- We personalize the store for each and every customer.
- We trade real estate for technology (which gets cheaper and more capable every year).
- We display customer reviews critical of our products.
- You can make a purchase with a few seconds and one click.
- We put used products next to new ones so you can choose.
- We share our prime real estate — our product detail pages — with third parties, and, if they can offer better value, we let them.

— Jeff Bezos

Source: AMZN 2004 Letter to shareholders
Published: Q1 2005

October 2

Capital efficiency of Amazon retail

"We have a cash generative operating cycle because we turn our inventory quickly, collecting payments from our customers before payments are due to suppliers. Our high inventory turnover means we maintain relatively low levels of investment in inventory - $480 million at year end on a sales base of nearly $7 billion.

The capital efficiency of our business model is illustrated by our modest investments in fixed assets, which were $246 million at year end or 4% of 2004 sales."

— Jeff Bezos

Source: 2004 Letter to shareholders
Published: April 2005

Capital Efficiency of Amazon Retail

"We have a cash generative operating cycle because we turn our inventory quickly, collecting payments from our customers before payments are due to suppliers. Our high inventory turnover means we maintain relatively low levels of investment in inventory — $480 million at year end on a sales base of nearly $7 billion.

The capital efficiency of our business model is illustrated by our modest investments in fixed assets, which were $246 million at year end or 4% of 2004 sales."

—**Jeff Bezos**

Source: The Film Archives   December 3, 2020
Published: April 2001

Get Big Fast

"If you look at what we've done over the past five years, we followed a strategy of Get Big Fast. Once you reach scale, you have to turn the focus from growth to operating efficiency.

At the time of our IPO, we had annualized sales of $60 million per year. At that scale, doing a bunch of hard work to improve operational efficiency by 1% nets you $600,000 of cost reduction.

Now [in 2001] we have annualized sales of $2.7 billion so that same work to improve efficiency would net $27 million of savings."

-Jeff Bezos

BONUS: Amazon's 2019 net revenue was $280 billion.

Source: The Film Archives
Published: April 2001

Get Big Fast

"If you look at what we've done over the past five years, we followed a strategy of *Get Big Fast*. Once you reach scale, you have to turn the focus from **growth** to **operating efficiency.**

At the time of our IPO, we had annualized sales of $60 million per year. At that scale, doing a bunch of hard work to improve operational efficiency by 1% nets you $600,000 of cost reduction.

Now [in 2001] we have annualized sales of $2.7 billion, so that same work to improve efficiency would net $27 million of savings."

-Jeff Bezos

Bonus: Amazon's 2019 net revenue was $280 billion.

Source: David Glick

Published: February 2020

The origins of tenets

According to David Glick who led the Pricing Software team, tenets originated at Amazon in 2006. To avoid rehashing previous decisions about pricing strategy, Jeff Bezos asked the team to summarize their strategy "So we remember what we decided last time."
And thus, tenets were born.

"While a team charter explains what a team does, a list of tenets explains how they do it."
    —Llew Mason, VP, Consumer Engagement

Pricing tenet #1 from 2006

We believe that by keeping our prices very, very low, we earn trust with customers over time, and that actually does maximize free cash flow over the long term.

Source: David Glick
Published: February 2020

The Origins of Tenets

According to David Glick who led the Pricing Software team, tenets originated at Amazon in 2006. To avoid rehashing previous decisions about pricing strategy, Jeff Bezos asked the team to summarize their strategy *"so we remember what we decided last time."* And thus, tenets were born.

"While a team charter explains what a team does, a list of tenets explains how they do it."

— Llew Mason, VP, Consumer Engagement

Pricing tenet #1 from 2006

We believe by keeping our prices very, very low, we earn trust with customers over time, and that actually does maximize free cash flow over the long term.

Tenets at Amazon

A tenet is a principle or belief that guide decision making. Tenets are not written in stone and include the catchphrase "unless you know better ones" because tenets evolve.

Tenets are either foundational describing why the team/product exists or aspirational describing how a team/product should operate, even if it doesn't do so today. Teams should try hard to have no more than 7 tenets.

Be memorable — the best tenets are easy to remember.

Source: AWS Cloud Enterprise Strategy Blog
Published: June 2018

Tenets at Amazon

A tenet is a principle or belief that guide decision making. Tenets are not written in stone and include the catchphrase "unless you know better ones" because tenets evolve. Tenets are either *foundational* describing why the team/product exists or *aspirational* which describe how a team/product intends to operate, even if it doesn't do so today. Teams should try hard to have no more than 7 tenets. Be memorable — the best tenets are easy to remember.

"The charter or mission states the what; the tenets state the how. Tenets are principles and core values that the program or team uses to fulfill the mission or charter."

—Joe Chung, AWS Enterprise Strategist & Evangelist

Fact of the Day 1's Tenets

1. Facts feature data with the source cited.
2. Content is digestible in under 60 seconds and encourages curiosity.
3. Topics rotate with a focus on the tech industry, business leadership, and thought-provoking ideas.
4. Using a whiteboard with handwritten facts is fun and personal.

Source: AMZN Letter to shareholders   May 7, 2020
Published: April 2008

The introduction of Kindle

"November 19, 2007, was a special day.
After three years of work, we introduced Amazon
Kindle to our customers. We did not expect
the level of demand that actually materialized.
We sold out in the first 5 1/2 hours, and
our supply chain and manufacturing
teams have had to scramble to increase
production capacity.

At the beginning of our design process,
we identified what we believe is the book's
most important feature. It disappears.
When you read a book, you don't notice
the paper and the ink and the glue and
the stitching. All of that dissolves, and
what remains is the author's world."

— Jeff Bezos

Source: AMZN Letter to shareholders
Published: April 2008

The Introduction of Kindle

"November 19, 2007, was a special day. After three years of work, we introduced Amazon Kindle to our customers. We did not expect the level of demand that actually materialized. We sold out in the first 5 1/2 hours, and our supply chain and manufacturing teams have had to scramble to increase production capacity.

At the beginning of our design process, we identified what we believe is the book's most important feature. It disappears. When you read a book, you don't notice the paper and the ink and the glue and the stitching. All of that dissolves, and what remains is the author's world."

— **Jeff Bezos**

Source: AMZN Letter to shareholders   January 13, 2020
Published: April 2012

Empower others to unleash their creativity

"The most radical of inventions are often those that empower others to unleash their creativity. With Amazon Web Services, Fulfillment by Amazon, and Kindle Direct Publishing we are creating self-service platforms that allow people to accomplish things that would otherwise be impossible.

These innovative, large-scale platforms are not zero-sum — they create win-win situations and create value for developers, entrepreneurs, customers, authors, and readers. I am emphasizing the self-service nature of these platforms because even well-meaning gatekeepers slow innovation. When a platform is self-service there's no expert gatekeeper ready to say "that will never work!""

— Jeff Bezos

Source: AMZN Letter to shareholders
Published: April 2012

Empower Others to Unleash Their Creativity

"The most radical of inventions are often those that empower **others** to unleash their creativity. With Amazon Web Services, Fulfillment by Amazon, and Kindle Direct Publishing we are creating self-service platforms that allow people to accomplish things that would otherwise be impossible.

These innovative, large-scale platforms are not zero-sum — they create win-win situations and create significant value for developers, entrepreneurs, customers, authors, and readers. I am emphasizing the self-service nature of these platforms because even well-meaning gatekeepers slow innovation. When a platform is self-service there's no expert gatekeeper ready to say that will never work!"

—**Jeff Bezos**

Source: New York Times   January 20, 2020

Published: December 2019

Amazon invents a shipping holiday

October 2014

Jeff Bezos sent Jeff Wilke an email:
How can we have a big annual sale
called Prime Day, and only Prime members
would be eligible?

November 2014

Project Piñata is presented to
the consumer leadership team.

January 2015

Bezos reviews the PRFAQ and gives
feedback:
Prime Day needs to be about one thing,
and we have to do it really well.
We have to have more deals than Black Friday.
(10,000+)

July 2015

Amazon launches the summer sales event
known as Prime Day.
Order growth is +18% compared to Black Friday
2014.

Source: New York Times
Published: December 2019

Amazon Invents a Shipping Holiday

October 2014: Jeff Bezos sent Jeff Wilke an email "How can we have a big annual sale called Prime Day, and only Prime members would be eligible?".

November 2014: Project Piñata is presented to the consumer leadership team.

January 2015: Bezos reviews the PRFAQ and gives feedback "Prime Day needs to be about one thing, and we have to do it really well. We have to have more deals than Black Friday (*10,000*)."

July 2015: Amazon launches the summer sales event known as Prime Day. Order growth *+18%* compared to Black Friday 2014.

Source: AMZN Shareholder Letter

Published: 2017

Businesses of Amazon

In the 2017 Shareholder Letter, Jeff Bezos reviews milestones across the following business units, in order:

Prime
AWS
Marketplace
Alexa
Amazon Devices
Prime Video
Amazon Music
Fashion
Whole Foods Market
Amazon Go
Treasure Truck
India
Sustainability
Empowering Small Businesses
Investment + Job Creation
Career Choice

Source: 2017 Shareholder Letter
Published: April 2018

Businesses of Amazon

Jeff Bezos reviews milestones of the following business units, in order:

- Prime
- AWS
- Marketplace
- Alexa
- Amazon Devices
- Prime Video
- Amazon Music
- Fashion
- Whole Foods
- Amazon Go
- Treasure Truck
- India
- Sustainability
- Empowering Small Business
- Investment & Job Creation
- Career Choice

Source: Fast Company
Published: April 2019

Amazon employee growth over time

1995	11
1997	614
1998	2,100
2000	9,000
2001	7,800
2002	7,500
2005	12,000
2007	17,000
2009	24,300
2011	56,200
2013	117,300
2014	154,100
2015	230,800
2017	566,000
2018	613,300

☐ = increasing yoy
☐ = decreasing yoy

Source: Fast Company
Published: April 2019

Amazon Employee Growth Over Time

1995: 11

1997: 614

1998: 2,100

2000: 9,000

2001: 7,800

2002: 7,500

2005: 12,000

2007: 17,000

2009: 24,300

2011: 56,200

2013: 117,300

2014: 154,100

2015: 230,800

2017: 566,000

2018: 613,300

Source: Vox
Published: May 2019

A timeline of Amazon Prime

2005 Launch of $79/year all-you-can-eat 2-day shipping

2006 Launch of Fulfillment by Amazon to allow sellers to pay Amazon to store and ship inventory

2013 USPS announces Sunday package delivery

2015 Prime Day created, an annual July event

2018 Minimum wage raises to $15/hour impacting 250,000 employees and 100,000 seasonal workers

2019 Prime shipping to move from 2-day to 1-day standard shipping with a $800M Q2 investment

Source: Vox
Published: May 2019

A Timeline of Amazon Prime

2005: Launch of *$79/year* all-you-can-eat 2-day shipping

2006: Launch of Fulfillment by Amazon to allow sellers to pay Amazon to store and ship inventory

2013: USPS announces Sunday package delivery

2015: Amazon creates Prime Day, an annual July event

2018: Minimum wage raises to *$15/hour* impacting *250,000* employees and *100,000* seasonal workers

2019: Prime Shipping to move from 2-day to 1-day standard shipping with a *$800M* investment in Q2

Source: r/Jokes
Published: November 2017

July 24, 2020

Monkeying around

What do you call two monkeys that share an Amazon account?

Prime mates

Source: Reddit, r/Jokes
Published: November 2017

Monkeying Around

What do you call two monkeys that share an Amazon account?

Prime mates.

Source: Various
Published: 2015 to 2019

Project Aerosmith

September 2015: Amazon leases four Boeing 767 freighters in an underused cargo airport in Ohio under the code name Project Aerosmith.

March 2016: Amazon acquires options to buy up to 19.9% of Air Transport International's stock and began scheduled operations with twenty 767 aircraft.

January 2017: Amazon announces that Prime Air would make Cincinnati/Northern Kentucky International Airport (CVG) its principal hub. There will be a 3M square feet sort center and parking space for 100+ cargo aircraft.

December 2017: Prime Air rebrands to Amazon Air. Prime Air now refers to the 30-minute delivery drone program.

December 2018: Amazon Air leases ten additional 767s, increasing the fleet to fifty aircraft.

June 2019: Amazon Air leases fifteen additional 737s.

"By 2021, Amazon Air will have a portfolio of 70 aircraft flying in our dedicated air network."
          — Dave Clark, SVP of WW Operations

Source: Air Cargo World, Times Gazette, Biz Journals, GeekWire, Amazon
Published: 2015–2019

Project Aerosmith

- **September 2015:** Amazon leases four Boeing 767 freighters in an underused cargo airport in Ohio under the code name Project Aerosmith.
- **March 2016:** Amazon acquires options to buy up to 19.9% of Air Transport International's stock and began scheduled operations with 20 Boeing 767 aircraft.
- **January 2017:** Amazon announces that Amazon Air would make Cincinnati/Northern Kentucky International Airport (CVG) its principal hub. There will be a 3M square feet sort center and a parking space for 100+ cargo aircraft.
- **December 2017:** Prime Air rebrands to Amazon Air. Note that now Amazon Prime Air refers to the 30-minute delivery drone program.
- **December 2018:** Amazon Air leases ten additional 767s, increasing the fleet to 50 aircraft.
- **June 2019:** Amazon Air leases fifteen additional 737s.

"By 2021, Amazon Air will have a portfolio of 70 aircraft flying in our dedicated air network."

— **Dave Clark, Senior Vice President Worldwide Operations at Amazon**

Source: Amazon
Date: DAY 1

Major Events in Amazon's History

Amazon founded	July 1994
IPO ($18/share)	May 1997
Amazon zShops	Sep. 1999
Me Marketplace	Nov. 2000
Super-saver shipping, $99+	Jan 2002
Prime, $79/year	Feb. 2005
Amazon Web Services	March 2006
Fulfillment by Amazon	Sep. 2006
Amazon Fresh	Aug. 2007
Kindle	Nov. 2007
Amazon Lockers	Sep. 2011
India Marketplace	June 2013
Amazon Echo	Nov. 2014
Whole Foods Acquisition	June 2017
140,000 Sellers surpass $100k in sales	Dec 2017
Fact of the Day 1 founded	Aug 2018

Source: Amazon — Wikipedia
Published: Day 1

Major Events in Amazon's History

- **Amazon founded** — July 1994
- **IPO ($18/share)** — May 1997
- **Amazon zShops** — Sep. 1999
- **M@ Marketplace** — Nov. 2000
- **Super-saver shipping, $99+** — Jan 2002
- **Prime** — Feb. 2005
- **Amazon Web Services** — March 2006
- **Fulfillment by Amazon** — Sep. 2006
- **AmazonFresh** — Aug. 2007
- **Kindle** — Nov. 2007
- **Amazon Lockers** — Sep. 2011
- **India Marketplace**– June 2013
- **Amazon Echo** — Nov. 2014
- **Whole Foods Acquisition** — June 2017
- **140,000 Sellers surpass $100k in sales** — Dec 2017
- *Fact of the Day 1* **founded** — Aug. 2018

Source: Amazon
Published: March 2020

Inventors at Amazon

A patent is a right granted to an inventor by the U.S. Patent and Trade Office that permits the inventor to exclude others from making, selling, or using the invention for a period of time. The U.S. patent system encourages unique and useful inventions.

Top 10 current Amazon employee inventors

1. Eric Jason Brandwine - 397
2. Brad Marshall - 200
3. Swaminathan Sivasubramanian- 193
4. David Richardson - 162
5. Darren Canavor - 122
6. Jeff Bezos - 120
7. Nicholas Allen - 114
8. Marc Brooker - 113
9. Kevin Miller - 103
10. Jaso Sorenson - 100

Amazon patent issuances

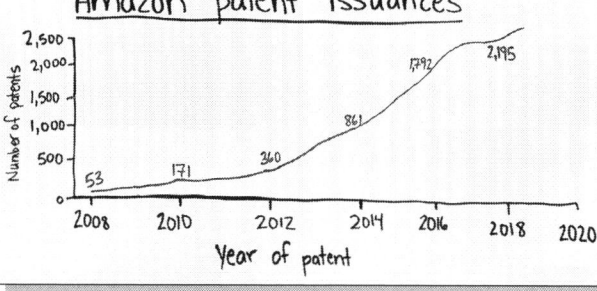

Source: Amazon
Published: March 2020

Inventors at Amazon

A patent is a right granted to an inventor by the U.S. Patent and Trade Office that permits the inventor to exclude others from making, selling, or using the invention for a period of time. The U.S. patent system encourages unique and useful inventions.

1. What technologies does Amazon tend to patent?

The state of investment in innovation at Amazon is strong. Customer obsession and innovation go hand in hand. Examples include Kindle, Fire TV, Echo, product recommendations, Prime Now, robotics, Prime Air, Amazon Go, and of course AWS.

2. Is there recognition for filing a patent?

Yes. Amazonians regularly get named on filings and receive recognition in a variety of forms. For filing a patent application, Amazonians receive an award shaped like a puzzle piece for each filing, and when a pending patent is approved—a process that can take about two years—a second customized blue puzzle piece with inventor name and patent number is awarded.

3. Who are the top 10 current Amazon employees with patents?

Eric Brandwine	397 patents
Brad Marshall	200 patents
Swaminathan Sivasubramanian	193 patents
David Richardson	162 patents
Darren Canavor	122 patents
Jeff Bezos	120 patents
Nicholas Allen	114 patents
Marc Brooker	113 patents
Kevin Miller	103 patents
Jaso Sorenson	100 patents

Source: Amazon Day 1 Blog
Published: October 2019

Amazon's Positions

We created these positions to provide customers, investors, policymakers, employees, and others our views on certain issues.

1. The federal minimum wage in the U.S. is too low and should be raised.

2. Human-induced climate change is real, serious, and action is needed from the public and private sectors.

3. The energy industry should have access to the same technologies as other industries.

4. Diversity and inclusion are good for business — and more fundamentally — simply right.

5. The rights of LGBTQ+ people must be protected.

6. We strongly support the rights of immigrants and immigration reform.

7. Governments at all levels — federal, state, and local — should have access to the best technology.

8. Governments should work quickly to put in place a regulatory framework for facial recognition technology.

9. Counterfeiters should receive stronger penalties under federal law.

10. Consumer data privacy should be protected under federal law.

11. Corporate tax codes should incentivize investment in the economy and job creation.

Source: Amazon Day 1 Blog
Published: October 2019

Amazon's Positions

"We created these positions to provide customers, investors, policymakers, employees, and others our views on certain issues. While our positions are carefully considered and deeply held, there is much room for healthy debate and differing opinions.

1. The federal minimum wage in the U.S. is too low and should be raised.
2. Human-induced climate change is real, serious, and action is needed from the public and private sectors.
3. The energy industry should have access to the same technologies as other industries.
4. Diversity and inclusion are good for business — and more fundamentally — simply right.
5. The rights of LGBTQ+ people must be protected.
6. We strongly support the rights of immigrants and immigration reform.
7. Governments at all levels — federal, state, and local — should have access to the best technology.
8. Governments should work quickly to put in place a regulatory framework for facial recognition technology.
9. Counterfeiters should receive stronger penalties under federal law.
10. Consumer data privacy should be protected under federal law.
11. Corporate tax codes should incentivize investment in the economy and job creation."

Source: Day 1 Blog
Published: March 2018

The story behind the building

Each building at Amazon has a peculiar name. Here are some of the buildings and the inspiration for the name.

Bigfoot: the tool used to map products on Amazon to titles on IMDb

Day 1: "This is Day 1 for the Internet,
  - and if we execute well, for Amazon.com."
  - — Jeff Bezos in the 1997 Letter to shareholders
  - Rumored to also be named after a daily email read by curious minds across the company, Fact of the Day 1.

Doppler: the code name for Amazon Echo

Houdini: the code name for Prime Now

Lowflyinghawk: an AWS customer's username on the AWS forums that was considered the "voice of the customer."

Obidos: the original page-rendering engine

re:Invent: yearly learning conference hosted by AWS

Rufus: Amazon's first dog, a corgi

Source: Day 1 Blog
Published: March 2018

The Story Behind the Building

Each building at Amazon has a peculiar name. Here are some of the buildings and the inspiration for the name:

Bigfoot: the tool used to map products on Amazon to titles on IMDb.

Day 1: "This is Day 1 for the Internet, and if we execute well, for Amazon.com" — Jeff Bezos in the 1997 Letter to shareholders. (Rumored to also be named after a daily email read by curious minds across the company, *Fact of the Day 1*).

Doppler: the code name for the Amazon Echo.

Houdini: the code name for Prime Now.

Lowflyinghawk: an AWS customer's username on the AWS forums that was considered the voice of the customer.

Obidos: the original page-rendering engine.

re:Invent: yearly learning conference hosted by AWS.

Rufus: Amazon's first dog, a corgi.

Source: Amazon Jobs
Published: October 2019

Come build the future with us

Right now there are more than 31,000 jobs posted to Amazon's career page.

Here are the top 5 teams, cities, and job categories.

Team	Open Jobs
Amazon Web Services	10,775
Retail	2,409
Fulfillment and Operations	1,674
Amazon Alexa	1,631
Human Resources	1,597

City	Open Jobs
Seattle, WA, USA	9,950
Bengaluru, Karnataka, IND	1,219
London, England, GBR	859
Herndon, Virginia, USA	802
New York, New York, USA	771

Job Category	Open Jobs
Software Development	8,862
Solutions Architect	2,865
PM, Non-Technical	2,047
Ops, IT, and Support Engineering	1,835
PM, Technical	1,809

Source: Amazon
Published: October 2019

Amazon hiring to build the future

As of October 31, 2019, there are more than *31,000* jobs posted to Amazon's career page. Here are the top 5 teams, cities, and job categories.

#	Team	Open Jobs
1	Amazon Web Services	10,775
2	Retail	2,409
3	Fulfillment & Operations	1,674
4	Amazon Alexa	1,631
5	Human Resources	1,597

#	City	Open Jobs
1	Seattle, Washington, USA	9,950
2	Bengaluru, Karnataka, IND	1,219
3	London, England, GBR	859
4	Herndon, Virginia, USA	802
5	New York, New York, USA	771

#	Job Category	Open Jobs
1	Software Development	8,862
2	Solutions Architect	2,865
3	PM, Non-Tech	2,047
4	Ops, IT, and Support Eng	1,835
5	PM, Tech	1,809

Source: Fortune
Published: May 2019

Amazon's Fortune 500 ranking

The Fortune 500 are the largest U.S. Corporations by revenue. Amazon has been part of the rankings since 2002. In 2018, Amazon ranked as #5 behind Walmart, Exxon Mobil, Apple, and Berkshire Hathaway.

year	Revenue $M	Revenue % Change yoy	Fortune 500 rank
1996	16	1500%	—
1998	610	312	—
2000	2,761	68	—
2002	3,933	26	492
2004	6,921	31	342
2006	10,711	26	272
2008	19,166	29	171
2010	34,204	40	78
2012	61,093	27	49
2014	89,045	20	29
2016	135,987	27	12
2018	232,887	31	5

00.9 (233 billion)

Source: Fortune
Published: May 2019

Amazon's Fortune 500 Ranking

The Fortune 500 are the largest United States corporations by revenue. Amazon has been part of the list since 2002. In 2018, Amazon ranked as #5, behind Walmart, Exxon Mobil, Apple, and Berkshire Hathaway.

Year	Revenue ($M)	Revenue % Change	Fortune 500 Rank
1995	1	-	-
1996	16	1500%	-
1997	148	825%	-
1998	610	312%	-
1999	1,640	169%	-
2000	2,761	68%	-
2001	3,122	13%	-
2002	3,933	26%	492
2003	5,264	34%	407
2004	6,921	31%	342
2005	8,490	23%	303
2006	10,711	26%	272
2007	14,835	39%	237
2008	19,166	29%	171
2009	24,509	28%	100
2010	34,204	40%	78
2011	48,077	41%	56
2012	61,093	27%	49
2013	74,452	22%	35
2014	89,045	20%	29
2015	107,066	20%	18
2016	135,987	27%	12
2017	177,866	31%	8
2018	232,887	31%	5

CHAPTER 2

JEFF BEZOS-ISMS

Source: Business Insider   November 25, 2020
Published: December 2014

My job as CEO of Amazon

"As the company has grown, my job has changed very much.
My main job today is working hard to help maintain the
culture of:

- insisting on high standards
- operational excellence and defect elimination
- inventiveness with a willingness to fail
- making bold experiments

Many of the traits are deeply ingrained in the culture,
I couldn't even change them at this point.
Cultures are self-reinforcing."

—Jeff Bezos

Source: Business Insider
Published: December 2014

My job as CEO of Amazon

"As the company has grown, my job has changed very much. My main job today is working hard to help maintain the culture of:

- insisting on high standards
- operational excellence and defect elimination
- inventiveness with a willingness to fail
- making bold experiments

Many of the traits are deeply ingrained in the culture, I couldn't even change them at this point. Cultures are self-reinforcing."

—**Jeff Bezos**

Source: AMZN Letter to shareholders   April 14, 2020
Published: April 2017

<u>Day 1 Vitality</u>

"There are many ways to center a business.
You can be competitor focused,
you can be product focused,
you can be technology focused,
you can be business model focused, and
there are more. But in my view,
obsessive customer focus is by far
the most protective of Day 1 vitality.

Why? There are many advantages to
a customer-centric approach, but here's
the big one:

Customers are always beautifully, wonderfully
dissatisfied, even when they report being
happy and business is great."

-Jeff Bezos

Source: AMZN Letter to shareholders
Published: April 2017

Day 1 Vitality

"There are many ways to center a business. You can be competitor focused, you can be product focused, you can be technology focused, you can be business model focused, and there are more. But in my view, obsessive customer focus is by far the most protective of Day 1 vitality.

Why? There are many advantages to a customer-centric approach, but here's the big one: customers are always beautifully, wonderfully dissatisfied, even when they report being happy and business is great."

— **Jeff Bezos**

Source: Chuck Severance
Published: December 2013

Jeff Bezos 1997 Interview

In June 1997 at the Special Libraries conference in Seattle, WA, Jeff Bezos was interviewed about his company Amazon.com.

Highlights from the five minute video:

- This is Day 1. This is the very beginning. This is the Kitty Hawk stage of electronic commerce.

- Books are incredibly unusual in one respect. There are more items in the book category than any other category by far... when you have that many items, you can build a store online that couldn't exist any other way.

- Attention is the scarce commodity of the late 20th century.

- Doing something new and innovative for the first time that adds real value for the customer is hard. If you do that, newspapers will write about you. Customers will tell other customers.

Source: Chuck Severance
Published: December 2013

"This is Day 1. This the very beginning." — Jeff Bezos

In June 1997 at the Special Libraries conference in Seattle, WA, Jeff Bezos was interviewed about his company Amazon.com.

Highlights from the five minute video:

- This is Day 1. This is the very beginning. This is the Kitty Hawk stage of electronic commerce.
- Books are incredibly unusual in one respect. There are more items in the book category than any other category by far... when you have that many items, you can build a store online that couldn't exist any other way.
- Attention is the scarce commodity of the late 20th century.
- Doing something new and innovative for the first time that adds real value for the customer is hard. If you do that, newspapers will write about you. Customers will tell other customers.

Source: Amazon Web Services   September 22, 2020
Published: November 2012

<u>Jeff Bezos's Pioneering Approach</u>

"When you attract people who have the DNA of pioneers and explorers, you build a company of like-minded people who want to invent. And that's what they think about when they get up in the morning.

How are we going to work backwards from customers and build a great product or service? That's the key element to invention. If you move about the world and think about how things can be improved, that's just fun.

Also essential for innovation is having a willingness to fail and a willingness to be misunderstood."

—Jeff Bezos

Source: Amazon Web Services
Published: November 2012

Jeff Bezos's Pioneering Approach

"When you attract people who have the DNA of pioneers and explorers, you build a company of like-minded people who want to invent. And that's what they think about when they get up in the morning.

How are we going to work backwards from customers and build a great product or service? That's the key element to invention. If you move about the world and think about how things can be improved, that's just fun.

Also essential for innovation is having a willingness to fail and a willingness to be misunderstood."

—**Jeff Bezos**

Source: AMZN 1998
Letter to Shareholders

November 23, 2020

Published: April 1999

Three questions to ask when hiring

In Amazon's 1998 letter to shareholders, Jeff Bezos wrote that setting the bar high in hiring was the most important element of Amazon's success: "It would be impossible to produce results in an environment as dynamic as the internet without extraordinary people."

As of 1999, during Amazon's hiring meetings, employees considered three questions before making a decision:

1. Will you admire this person?

2. Will this person raise the average level of effectiveness of the group they're entering?

3. Along what dimension might this person be a superstar?

Source: AMZN 1998 Letter to Shareholders
Published: April 1999

Three questions to ask when hiring

In Amazon's 1998 letter to shareholders, Jeff Bezos wrote that setting the bar high in hiring was the most important element of Amazon's success: *"It would be impossible to produce results in an environment as dynamic as the Internet without extraordinary people."*

As of 1999, during Amazon's hiring meetings, employees considered three questions before making a decision:

1. Will you admire this person?
2. Will this person raise the average level of effectiveness of the group they're entering?
3. Along what dimension might this person be a superstar?

Source: Amazon Shareholder Letter
Published: 1997

It's not easy to work here

When I interview people I tell them,
"you can work long, hard, or smart,
but at Amazon you can't choose two out of the three",
but we are working to build something important,
Something that matters to our customers,
Something that we can all tell our
grandchildren about. Such things aren't meant to be easy.

Source: 1996 Letter to shareholders
Published: April 1997

We are working to build something important

It's not easy to work here. When I interview people I tell them, **"You can work long, hard, or smart, but at Amazon.com you can't choose two out of three"**, but we are working to build something important, something that matters to our customers, something that we can all tell our grandchildren about. Such things aren't meant to be easy.

— **Jeff Bezos**

Source: AMZN 1998 Letter to shareholders
Published: Q1 1999

Wake up every morning terrified

" We intend to build the world's most customer-centric company. But there is no rest for the weary. I constantly remind our employees to be afraid, to wake up every morning terrified. Not of our competition, but of our customers.

We consider our customers to be loyal to us — right up until the second that someone else offers them a better service.

    — Jeff Bezos

Source: 1998 Letter to shareholders
Published: April 1999

Ambitions towards customer-centricity

"We intend to build the world's most customer-centric company. But there is no rest for the weary. I constantly remind our employees to be afraid, to wake up every morning terrified. Not of our competition, but of our customers. We consider customers to be loyal to us — right up until the second that someone else offers them a better service."

— **Jeff Bezos**

Source: Amazon   September 16, 2020
Published: April 2018

Expectations are a Moving Target

In the 2017 Letter to Amazon Shareholders, Jeff Bezos writes:

"One thing I love about customers is that they are divinely discontent. Their expectations are never static – they go up... People have a voracious appetite for a better way, and yesterday's 'wow' quickly becomes today's 'ordinary'. I see that cycle of improvement happening at a faster rate than ever before... You cannot rest on your laurels in this world. Customers won't have it."

Source: 2017 Letter to shareholders
Published: April 2018

Expectations are a Moving Target

"One thing I love about customers is that they are divinely discontent. Their expectations are never static — they go up… People have a voracious appetite for a better way, and yesterday's 'wow' quickly becomes today's 'ordinary.' I see that cycle of improvement happening at a faster rate than ever before… You cannot rest on your laurels in this world. Customers won't have it."

— Jeff Bezos

Source: 2014 Letter to Shareholders
Published: Q1 2015

Don't just swipe right, get married

A dreamy business offering has at least four characteristics

1) Customers love it
2) It can grow to very large size
3) It has strong returns on capital
4) It's durable with time — with the potential to endure for decades

When you find one of these, don't just swipe right, get married.

We are now happily wed to what I believe are three such life partners:

Marketplace
Prime
AWS

Source: 2014 Letter to shareholders
Published: April 2015

Don't just swipe right, get married

A dreamy business offering has at least four characteristics. Customers love it, it can grow to a very large size, it has strong returns on capital, and it's durable in time — with the potential to endure for decades. When you find one of these, don't just swipe right, get married. We are now happily wed to what I believe are three such life partners: *Marketplace*, *Prime*, and *AWS*.

— Jeff Bezos

Source: David Rubenstein
Published: September 2018

Executive decision making at Amazon

"As a senior executive, what do you really get paid to do? You get paid to make a small number of high quality decisions. Your job is <u>not</u> to make thousands of decisions every day.

All of the Amazon senior executives are similar in that they work and live in the future. They do not focus on the current quarter.

Right now, I'm working on a quarter that will reveal itself 3 years from now. If I make 3 good decisions a day, that's enough. They should be as high quality as I can make them."

— Jeff Bezos

Source: David Rubenstein
Published: September 2018

Executive decision making at Amazon

"As a senior executive, what do you really get paid to do? You get paid to make a small number of high quality decisions. Your job is not to make thousands of decisions every day.

All of the Amazon senior executives are similar in that they work and live in the future. They do not focus on the current quarter.

Right now, I'm working on a quarter that will reveal it-self 3 years from now. If I make 3 good decisions a day, that's enough. They should be as high quality as I can make them."

—**Jeff Bezos**

Source: AMZN Letter to Shareholders   February 21, 2020
Published: April 2007

Why Amazon can start businesses from scratch

Amazon's culture is unusually supportive of small businesses with big potential, and Jeff Bezos believes it's a source of competitive advantage.

"I remember how excited we were in 1996 as we crossed $10 million in book sales. Today, when a new business inside Amazon grows to $10 million, we grow from $10 billion to $10.01 billion. It would be easy for the senior executives who run our established billion dollar businesses to scoff. But they don't. They watch the growth rates of the emerging businesses and send emails of congratulations. That's pretty cool, and we're proud it's a part of our culture."

-Jeff Bezos

Source: AMZN Letter to shareholders
Published: April 2007

Why Amazon Can Start Businesses From Scratch

Amazon's culture is unusually supportive of small businesses with big potential, and Jeff Bezos believes that it's a source of competitive advantage.

"I remember how excited we were in 1996 as we crossed $10 million in book sales. Today, when a new business inside Amazon grows to $10 million, we grow from $10 billion to $10.01 billion. It would be easy for the senior executives who run our established billion dollar businesses to scoff. But they don't. They watch the growth rates of the emerging businesses and send emails of congratulations. That's pretty cool, and we're proud it's a part of our culture."

— **Jeff Bezos**

Source: Geekwire   February 28, 2020
Published: June 2011

Stubborn on vision and flexible on details

Question: Amazon seems to be executing well lately — is the company taking enough risks? If it's still Amazon's philosophy to make bold bets, I would expect that maybe some of them wouldn't work out, but I am not seeing that. So, my question is Where are all the losers?

Answer by Jeff Bezos: In a way, that is like the nicest compliment I've ever gotten. I can guarantee you that everything we do will not work. I am never concerned about that because we are stubborn on vision and flexible on details. We don't give up on things easily.

Our third-party seller business is an example of that. It took us three tries to get the third-party seller business to work — Amazon Auctions, zShops, and Amazon Marketplace. We didn't give up.

Source: Geekwire
Published: June 2011

Stubborn on Vision and Flexible on Details

Question: Amazon seems to be executing well lately — is the company taking enough risks? If it's still Amazon's philosophy to make bold bets, I would expect that maybe some of them wouldn't work out, but I am not seeing that. So, my question is where are all the losers?

Answer by Jeff Bezos: In a way, that is like the nicest compliment I've ever gotten. I can guarantee you that everything we do will not work. I am never concerned about that because we are stubborn on vision and flexible on details. We don't give up on things easily.

Our third-party seller business is an example of that. It took us three tries to get the third-party seller business to work (Amazon Auctions, zShops, Amazon Marketplace). We didn't give up.

Source: The Bush Center   October 13, 2020
Published: April 2018

When We are Criticized

"What I preach at Amazon to all of our employees is that when we are criticized, there is a simple process that you need to go through.

First, you look yourself in the mirror and decide, is your critic right? Do you agree? Are we doing something wrong? If you are, change!

If you look yourself in the mirror and decide that your critic is wrong, then do not change. Do the right thing and have a deep keel."

-Jeff Bezos

Source: The Bush Center
Published: April 2018

When We are Criticized

"What I preach at Amazon to all of our employees is that when we are criticized, there is a simple process that you need to go through.

First, you look yourself in the mirror and decide, is your critic right? Do you agree? Are we doing something wrong? If you are, change!

If you look yourself in the mirror and decide that your critic is wrong, then do not change. Do the right thing and have a deep keel."

—**Jeff Bezos**

Source: AMZN Letter to shareholders
Published: April 2013

<u>Voting machine versus weighing machine</u>

"As I write this, our recent stock performance has been positive, but we constantly remind ourselves of an important point —
as I frequently quote famed investor Benjamin Graham in our employee all-hands meetings —

"In the short run, the market is a voting machine but in the long run, the market is a weighing machine."

We don't celebrate a 10% increase in the stock price like we celebrate excellent customer experience. We aren't 10% smarter when that happens and conversely aren't 10% dumber when the stock goes the other way.

We want to be weighed, and we're always working to build a heavier company."

— Jeff Bezos

Source: AMZN Letter to shareholders
Published: April 2013

Voting Machine Versus Weighing Machine

"As I write this, our recent stock performance has been positive, but we constantly remind ourselves of an important point — as I frequently quote famed investor Benjamin Graham in our employee all-hands meetings — "In the short run, the market is a voting machine but in the long run, it is a weighing machine."

We don't celebrate a 10% increase in the stock price like we celebrate excellent customer experience. We aren't 10% smarter when that happens and conversely aren't 10% dumber when the stock goes the other way.

We want to be weighed, and we're always working to build a heavier company."

—**Jeff Bezos**

Source: The Bush Center   November 4, 2020
Published: April 2018

A precursor to taking risks

"If you're an entrepreneur, you take risks. One of the foundational things to be able to take risks is to have support... from mentors or from somebody who loves you. This builds up and allows you to jump off into uncharted terrain and enables you to do something new.

I certainly had this support system when I started Amazon. Somebody has to step into your life and provide this kind of support, whether from a parent, grandparent, family friend, or a teacher."

-Jeff Bezos

Source: The Bush Center
Published: April 2018

A precursor to taking risks

"If you're an entrepreneur, you take risks. One of the foundational things to be able to take risks is to have support ... from mentors or from somebody who loves you. This builds up and allows you to jump off into uncharted terrain and enables you to do something new.

I certainly had this support system when I started Amazon. Somebody has to step into your life and provide this kind of support, whether from a parent, grandparent, family friend, or a teacher."

— **Jeff Bezos**

Source: David Rubenstein   September 2, 2020
Published: September 2018

I've Seen Small Things Get Big

The Bezos Day One Fund funded with $2 billion has two priorities:

#1 Day 1 Families Fund: traditional grant giving to provide shelter and hunger support to address the immediate needs of young families.

#2 Day 1 Academies Fund: building a non-profit organization to launch and operate a network of high-quality, full-scholarship Montessori-inspired preschools in underserved communities.

"It is Day 1. Everything that I've ever done has started small. Amazon started with a couple of people. Blue Origin started with five people and a small budget. Now the budget at Blue Origin is over $1 billion each year. I've seen small things get big. It is part of this Day 1 mentality. Even though Amazon is a large company, I want it to have the heart and spirit of a small one." -Jeff Bezos

Source: David Rubenstein
Published: September 2018

I've Seen Small Things Get Big

The Bezos Day One Fund funded with $2 billion has two priorities:

(1) **Day 1 Families Fund**: traditional grant giving to provide shelter and hunger support to address the immediate needs of young families.

(2) **Day 1 Academies Fund**: building a non-profit organization to launch and operate a network of high-quality, full-scholarship Montessori-inspired preschools in underserved communities.

"It is Day 1. Everything that I've ever done has started small. Amazon started with a couple of people. Blue Origin started with five people and a small budget. Now the budget at Blue Origin is over $1 billion each year. I've seen small things get big. It is part of this Day 1 mentality. Even though Amazon is a large company, I want it to have the heart and spirit of a small one."

— Jeff Bezos

Source: Long Now
Published: February 2018

April 3, 2020

The 10,000 year clock

In the mountains of Texas, there is a 500 foot (150 meters) tall Clock built to run for 10,000 years. It is designed to be a symbol of long-term thinking.

The clock's creation is funded by Jeff Bezos, CEO of Amazon, and is built on his property. The clock is currently under construction and does not have a completion date scheduled. It is planned to be open to the public once it is ready.

Source: Long Now
Published: February 2018

The 10,000 Year Clock

In the mountains of Texas, there is a 500 foot (150 meters) tall clock built to run for 10,000 years. It is designed to be a symbol of long-term thinking.

The clock's creation is funded by Jeff Bezos, CEO of Amazon, and is built on his property. The clock is currently under construction and does not have a completion date scheduled. It is planned to be open to the public once it is ready.

CHAPTER 3

CULTURE OF INNOVATION

Source: The Film Archives   November 11, 2020

Published: April 2001

Customer-centricity at Amazon

Interviewer: "You make a big deal about having a customer-centric focus. Do you honestly believe that the customer is always right?"

Jeff Bezos: "Our mission is to be Earth's most customer-centric company. We have a precise definition of customer-centric that includes three things:

- Listen: the most traditional meaning of customer-centric; if you don't listen to your customers, you will fail; for example, a focus group
- Invent: often involves not listening to your customers; it isn't the customer's job to invent for themselves
- Personalize: putting the customer at the center of their own universe; redecorating the store for each individual customer"

Source: The Film Archives
Published: April 2001

Customer-centricity at Amazon

Interviewer: "You make a big deal about having a customer-centric focus. Do you honestly believe that the customer is always right?"

Jeff Bezos: "Our mission is to be Earth's most customer-centric company. We have a precise definition of customer-centric that includes three things:

- **Listen:** the most traditional meaning of customer-centric; if you don't listen to your customers, you will fail; for example, a focus group
- **Invent:** often involves not listening to your customers; it isn't the customer's job to invent for themselves
- **Personalize:** putting the customer at the center of their own universe; redecorating the store for each individual customer"

Source: Internet Association   November 18, 2020
Published: May 2017

Amazon's Approach

"The common thread [between Amazon's businesses] is an approach. We have a very distinctive approach that we have been honing and refining for 22 years.

1. Customer Obsession instead of, for example, competitor obsession, technology obsession, product obsession, or business model obsession. Not just listening to customers, but inventing on their behalf.

2. Eager to invent and pioneer because customers are always dissatisfied, even when they think they're happy. They actually do want a better way but don't know yet what that should be.

3. Long-term oriented thinking in 5 to 7-year time frames. If you start to think that way, it changes how you spend your time and improves your ability to look around corners."

-Jeff Bezos

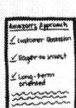

Source: Internet Association
Published: May 2017

Amazon's Approach

"The common thread [between Amazon's businesses] is an approach. We have a very distinctive approach that we have been honing and refining for 22 years.

1. Customer Obsession instead of, for example, competitor obsession, technology obsession, product obsession, or business model obsession. Not just listening to customers, but inventing on their behalf.
2. Eager to invent and pioneer because customers are always dissatisfied, even when they think they're happy. They actually do want a better way but don't know yet what that should be.
3. Long-term oriented thinking in 5 to 7-year time frames. If you start to think that way, it changes how you spend your time and improves your ability to look around corners."

- Jeff Bezos

Source: Wall Street Journal   August 28, 2020
Published: October 2011

Amazon Two-Pizza Teams

Founding Amazon, Jeff Bezos wanted a decentralized, even disorganized company where independent ideas would prevail over groupthink.

He instituted, as a company-wide rule, the concept of the "two-pizza team":
any team should be small enough that it could be fed with two pizzas.

The more people you pack into a team, the less productive the meetings of that team will likely be.

For each additional person over seven members in a decision making group, decision effectiveness is reduced by approximately 10%.
(source: Bain + Company)

Source: Wall Street Journal
Published: October 2011

Amazon Two-Pizza Teams

Founding Amazon, Jeff Bezos wanted a decentralized, even disorganized company where independent ideas would prevail over groupthink.

He instituted, as a company-wide rule, the concept of the *"two-pizza team"*: any team should be small enough that it could be fed with two pizzas.

The more people you pack into a team, the less productive the meetings of that team will likely be.

For each additional person over seven members in a decision-making group, decision effectiveness is reduced by approximately *10%* (source: Bain & Company).

Source: AMZN Letter to shareholders   January 31, 2020
Published: April 2011

Service-oriented architecture (SOA)

At Amazon, our technologies are almost exclusively implemented as services. SOA allows for plugging in new services or upgrade existing services in a granular fashion to address new business requirements.

" Our e-commerce platform is composed of hundreds of software services that work in concert to deliver functionality ranging from recommendations to order fulfillment to inventory tracking. Services evolve at their own pace without impacting the other components of the overall system.

For example, to construct a product detail page for a customer visiting Amazon.com, our software calls on between 200 and 300 services to present a highly personalized experience for that customer. "

- Jeff Bezos

Source: AMZN Letter to shareholders
Published: April 2011

Service-Oriented Architecture

At Amazon, our technologies are almost exclusively implemented as services. Service-oriented architecture (SOA) allows for plugging in new services or upgrade existing services in a granular fashion to address new business requirements.

"Our ecommerce platform is composed of a federation of hundreds of software services that work in concert to deliver functionality ranging from recommendations to order fulfillment to inventory tracking. Services evolve at their own pace without impacting the other components of the overall system.

For example, to construct a product detail page for a customer visiting Amazon.com, our software calls on between 200 and 300 services to present a highly personalized experience for that customer."

—Jeff Bezos

Working Backwards at Amazon

"The Working Backwards process is a huge amount of work. But, it will save you even more work later on." - Jeff Bezos

We begin the process of Working Backwards with 5 questions:

1. Who is the customer?
   ↳ consider the time, place, and situation.

2. What is the customer problem or opportunity?
   ↳ Specify a problem you are going to solve.
   ↳ Define the size of the problem.

3. What is the most important customer benefit?
   ↳ Prioritize what the customer values.

4. How do you know what customers want or need?
   ↳ Recognize that your personal experiences may not be representative of customers.
   ↳ Challenge yourself to use data to back your thinking.

5. What does the customer experience look like?
   ↳ Whiteboard sketch
   ↳ Storyboard
   ↳ User journey map
   ↳ Wireframe
   ↳ Technical architecture diagram

Source: Amazon Web Services
Published: April 2019

Working Backwards at Amazon

"The Working Backwards process is a huge amount of work. But, it will save you even more work later on." — Jeff Bezos

We begin the process of Working Backwards with 5 questions:

1. **Who is the customer?**
   - Consider the time, place, and situation
2. **What is the customer problem or opportunity?**
   - Specify a problem you are going to solve. Define the size of the problem.
3. **What is the most important customer benefit?**
   - Prioritize what the customer values.
4. **How do you know what customers want or need?**
   - Recognize that your personal experience may not be representative of customers.
   - Challenge yourself to use data to back your thinking.
5. **What does the customer experience look like?**
   - Whiteboard sketch
   - Storyboard
   - User journey map
   - Wireframe
   - Technical architecture diagram

How we write a Working Backwards document (yesterday's fact)

After we answer the 5 Working Backwards questions, we write a document inclusive of the following three elements:

I. Press release (PR)
- One-page narrative describing a new product, service, or feature at a high-level
- Describes the vision
- Written using customer-centric language
- Any Amazonian should be able to understand the idea. Remember to spell out acronyms the first time they're used!
- Use a customer testimonial to reinforce why the customer cares about what you're launching

2. Frequently asked questions (FAQs)
- Multi-page questions and answers that a customer or Amazonian may ask after reading the PR
- Describes implementation details, data, and risks
- Examples of customer FAQs:
  - i. How much will this cost?
  - ii. Where can I find this?
  - iii. How do I cancel if I change my mind?
- Examples of Amazonian FAQs
  - iv. What is the underlying technology?
  - v. How does this support our goals?
  - vi. How can we launch this more quickly?

3. Visuals to help communicate an idea (Appendix)
- Use visuals to show how customers will discover the product and what they will be able to do with it
- Describes how a product feels
- Start with a hand-drawn visual, not a high-fidelity mockup

Source: Amazon Web Services
Published: April 2018

How We Write a Working Backwards Document

After we answer the 5 Working Backwards questions, we write a document inclusive of 3 components:

1. **Press Release (PR)**
    a. One-page narrative describing a new product, service, or feature at a high-level.

    b. Describes the vision.

    c. Written using customer-centric language.

    d. Any Amazonian should be able to understand the idea (spell out your acronyms the first time they're used).

    e. Use a customer testimonial to reinforce why the customer cares about what you're launching.

2. **Frequently Asked Questions (FAQs)**
    a. Multi-page questions and answers that a customer or Amazonian may ask after reading.

    b. Describes implementation details, data, and risks.

    c. Examples of customer FAQs:

    i.   How much will this cost?

    ii. Where can I find this?

    iii. How do I cancel if I change my mind?

    d. Example of Amazonian FAQs:

    i.   What is the underlying technology?

    ii. How does this support our goals?

    iii. How can we launch this more quickly?

3. **Visuals to help communicate an idea (Appendix)**
    a. Use visuals to show how customers will discover the product and what they will be able to do with it.

    b. Describes how a product feels.

    c. Start with a hand-drawn visual, not a high-fidelity mockup.

Source: AMZN 2015 Letter to shareholders

November 17, 2020

Published: April 2016

One-way and Two-way Doors

One-way doors: decisions that are consequential and nearly irreversible; should be made methodically, carefully, slowly, with great deliberation and consultation.

Two-way doors: decisions that are changeable and reversible; should be made quickly by high judgment individuals or small groups. If you've made a suboptimal decision, you can reopen the door and go back through.

"As organizations get larger, there seems to be a tendency to use the heavy-weight [one-way door] decision-making process on most decisions, including many [two-way door] decisions. The end result of this is slowness, unthoughtful risk aversion failure to experiment sufficiently, and consequently diminished invention. We'll have to figure out how to fight that tendency."

-Jeff Bezos

Source: AMZN 2015 Letter to shareholders
Published: April 2016

One-way and Two-way Doors

One-way doors: decisions that are consequential and nearly irreversible; should be made methodically, carefully, slowly, with great deliberation and consultation.

Two-way doors: decisions that are changeable and reversible; should be made quickly by high judgment individuals or small groups. If you've made a suboptimal decision, you can reopen the door and go back through.

"As organizations get larger, there seems to be a tendency to use the heavy-weight [one-way door] decision-making process on most decisions, including many [two-way door] decisions. The end result of this is slowness, unthoughtful risk aversion, failure to experiment sufficiently, and consequently diminished invention. We'll have to figure out how to fight that tendency."

-**Jeff Bezos**

Source: Brad Porter, VP at Amazon
Published: September 2015

The Beauty of Amazon's 6-Pager

An Amazon meeting driven by a 6-pager is magical.
The down side to the 6-pager is that writing a good
6-page evidence-based narrative is hard work.
The preparation required to write a good 6-pager does two things:

(1) It requires the team to deeply understand their
own business, gather their data, understand their
operating tenets, and be able to communicate
them clearly.

(2) A great document enables our senior executives
to internalize a whole new space they may
not be familiar with in 30 minutes of reading.

Outsiders sometimes look at Amazon and wonder
how Amazon can possibly focus on so many
different businesses at once.
The answer is that Amazon has fundamentally innovated
in how to scale the process of bringing groups
of people deeply up to speed in new spaces
and making critical decisions based on
that insight quickly.

Source: Brad Porter, former VP at Amazon
Published: September 2015

The Beauty of Amazon's 6-Pager

An Amazon meeting driven by a 6-pager is magical.

The down side to the 6-pager is that writing a good 6-page evidence-based narrative is hard work.

The preparation required to write a good 6-pager does two things:

1. It requires the team to deeply understand their own space, gather their data, understand their operating tenets and be able to communicate them clearly.
2. A great document enables our senior executives to internalize a whole new space they may not be familiar with in 30 minutes of reading.

Outsiders sometimes look at Amazon and wonder how Amazon can possibly focus on so many different businesses at once. The answer is that Amazon has fundamentally innovated in how to scale the process of bringing groups of people deeply up to speed in new spaces and making critical decisions based on that insight quickly.

Source: Gallup
Published: December 2017

Good intentions never work

"A lot of people have great intentions, but at Amazon, we work to build mechanisms so that we can take those intentions and turn them into complete processes that we implement and inspect." - Beth Galetti, SVP of HR

One of our mechanisms is our interview process. It's set up to evaluate a candidate from the standpoint of the Leadership Principles. Each interview loop includes a Bar Raiser, an Amazonian who is an objective third party not associated with the team. The best long-term hiring decisions are made to ensure the company is always serving, surprising, and innovating on behalf of customers.

The role of the Bar Raiser is to be a steward of Amazon's 14 Leadership Principles.

Bar Raisers - since 1999 - aren't motivated to hire fast; they are motivated to hire well.

Source: Gallup
Published: December 2017

Good Intentions Never Work

"A lot of people have great intentions, but at Amazon, we work to build mechanisms so that we can take those intentions and turn them into complete processes that we implement and inspect."

—Beth Galetti, Senior Vice President
of Human Resources at Amazon

One of our mechanisms is our interview process. It's set up to evaluate a candidate from the standpoint of our Leadership Principles. Each interview loop includes a *"Bar Raiser,"* an Amazonian who is an objective third party not associated with the team. The best long-term hiring decisions are made to ensure the company is always serving, surprising, and innovating for customers.

The role of the Bar Raiser is to be a steward of Amazon's 14 Leadership Principles. Bar Raisers — *since 1999* — aren't motivated to hire fast; they are motivated to hire well.

Source: Harvard Business Review

Published: October 2007

Experimentation at Amazon

"What you really want to do companywide is maximize the number of experiments you can do per given unit of time. Since the outcomes of all these things are uncertain, if you can figure out how to conduct an experiment, you can make more bets. So, the key, really, is reducing the cost of the experiments.

We have a group called Weblab that allows teams at Amazon to constantly experiment with the user interface on the website. Weblab is a huge labratory for us, allowing for very low cost experiments so that we can run a much larger number of them."

-Jeff Bezos

Source: Harvard Business Review
Published: October 2007

Experimentation at Amazon

"What you really want to do company-wide is maximize the number of experiments you can do per given unit of time. Since the outcomes of all these things are uncertain, if you can figure out how to conduct an experiment, you can make more bets. So the key, really, is reducing the cost of the experiments.

We have a group called Weblab that allows teams at Amazon to constantly experiment with the user interface on the website. Weblab is a huge laboratory for us, and we've put a lot of energy into trying to figure out how to be very low cost with those experiments so that we can run a much larger number of them."

—**Jeff Bezos**

Source: Success Principles
Published: March 2018

Amazon Failures to learn from

Amazon Webstore – Shopify competitor
Amazon Destinations – hotel booking service
Endless.com – a high-end fashion site
WebPay – PayPal competitor
Askville – Question-and-answer site
Amazon Auction – eBay competitor
Fire Phone – iPhone competitor

"If you know in advance an experiment
is going to work, it's not an experiment."
— Jeff Bezos, 2015 Letter to Shareholders

Source: Success Principles
Published: March 2018

Amazon Failures To Learn From

- Amazon Webstore (think Shopify)
- Amazon Destinations (think TripAdvisor)
- Endless.com (think Zappos)
- WebPay (think PayPal)
- Askville (think Yahoo Answers)
- AmazonAuction (think eBay)
- Fire Phone (think iPhone)

"If you know in advance an experiment is going to work, it's not an experiment."

—Jeff Bezos

Source: Wall Street Journal
Published: October 2017

An interview with Jeff Wilke

Question: Amazon encourages employees to fail big. Tell us about a big, fall-on-your-face failure.

Answer: When we were deciding whether to do Kindle, Jeff Bezos presented his idea to Amazon's board of directors. I thought that we should not do it because we were a software company that did not know anything about hardware.
At this time, Jeff Bezos said it is the right thing to do for customers.
I disagreed and committed, and I'm very glad I did.

Question: What would you say to people who say that Amazon is too big?

Answer: I think there's a big difference between horizontal breadth and vertical depth. Across our businesses we face incredible competition. We think our job is to keep inventing for customers.

How he works

- How many unread emails are in your inbox? Probably 70.
- The one trait you look for in a hire? Competence
- What is your favorite email list? Fact of the Day!

Okay, we may have added this one. #aspirational

Source: *Wall Street Journal*
Published: October 2017

An interview with Jeff Wilke

Question: Amazon encourages employees to fail big. Tell us about a big, fall-on-your-face failure.

Answer: When we were deciding whether to do Kindle, Jeff Bezos presented his idea to Amazon's board of directors. I thought that we should not do it because we were a software company that did not know anything about hardware. At the time, Jeff Bezos said it is the right thing to do for customers. I disagreed and committed, and I'm very glad I did.

Question: What would you say to people who say that Amazon is too big?

Answer: I think there's a big difference between horizontal breadth and vertical depth. Across our businesses we face incredible competition. We think our job is to keep inventing for customers.

How he works:
- **How many unread emails are in your inbox?** Probably 70.
- **The one trait you look for in a hire is?** Competence.
- **What is your favorite email list?** *Fact of the Day 1* (... okay this one is aspirational!)

.

CHAPTER 4

HOW THEY BUILT THIS

Source: Google and TED
Published: December 2011

Massive scale online collaboration

CAPTCHA (2003)

- A challenge-response test used in computing to determine whether or not a user is human.
- Letters and numbers distorted as squiggly characters

  Example: $\chi_g \mathcal{3} T$ = d g 3 T
- 200M per day answered as of 2009 ∘ ∘ ∘ (At 10 seconds each, 500,000 hours daily)

reCAPTCHA (2007)

- A company that uses CAPTCHA to perform useful tasks like preserve books, improve maps, and build machine-learning training data

- Example of a task: digitize scanned books by asking humans to type words that the computer could not recognize

- Acquired by Google in September 2009

- Why you'll often get 2 words:

  1) Verify: a word the system knows the answer to and assumes you're human if you can confirm it.

  2) Decode: a word the system doesn't know. It won't grade you for this answer. You and others are asked the same word which contribute to the computer's knowledge by crowd sourcing the answer.

Invisible reCAPTCHA (2018)

☐ I'm not a robot

- Doesn't present any human verification visually
- Monitors user actions (eg. cursor movements, rate of scrolling)
- Returns a score which represents the probability if the user is a human or a bot

Source: Google & TED
Published: December 2011

Massive Scale Online Collaboration

CAPTCHA (2003)

- A challenge-response test used in computing to determine whether or not the user is human.
- Letters and numbers distorted as squiggly characters (e.g., dG3T).
- *200M* per day as of 2009 at *10 seconds* each, totaling *500K* man-hours everyday.

reCAPTCHA (2007)

- A company that uses CAPTCHA to perform useful tasks like preserve books, improve maps, and build machine-learning training data.
- Example of a task: digitize scanned books by asking humans to type words that the computer could not recognize.
- Acquired by Google in September 2009.
- Why you'll often get 2 words.
    - **Verify:** a word the system knows the answer to and assumes you're human if you can confirm it.
    - **Decode:** a word the system doesn't know. It won't grade you for this answer. You and others are asked the same word which contribute to the computer's knowledge by crowdsourcing the answer.

Invisible reCAPTCHA (2018)

- Doesn't present any human verification visually.
- Monitors user actions (e.g., cursor movements, rate of scrolling).
- Returns a score which represents the probability if the user is a human or a bot.

Source: Visual Capatalist
Published: January 2019

May 10

The growth of the dollar store

Between 2007 and 2017, over 11,000 new dollar stores were opened in the U.S.

That's 93/month or 3/day.

A dollar store costs $250k to launch a new store, while a Walmart costs $15M.

Source: Visual Capitalist
Published: January 2019

The Growth of the Dollar Store

Between 2007 and 2017, over *11,000* new dollar stores were opened; that's roughly *93* new stores a month, or *3* per day. A dollar store costs *$250k* to launch a new store while a Walmart costs *$15M*.

Source: Lenny Rachitsky
Published: May 2020

The story of DoorDash

The very first iteration of DoorDash was a website called PaloAltoDelivery.com with PDF'd menus of restaurants in Palo Alto, California.
To reach customers, Tony Xu and the team printed flyers and put them all over Stanford University.

The team first wanted to see if there was demand when they charged $6 for delivery.

That was how it all started. A website with PDF menus and flyers.

Now, DoorDash has raised $2.5 billion and is the largest US meal-delivery company.

Big things start small.

Source: Lenny Rachitsky
Published: May 2020

The story of DoorDash

The very first iteration of DoorDash was a website called **PaloAltoDelivery.com** with PDF'd menus of restaurants in Palo Alto, California. To reach customers, **Tony Xu** and the team printed flyers and put them all over Stanford University. The team first wanted to see if there was demand when they charged $6 for delivery. That was how it all started. A website with PDF menus and flyers.

Now, DoorDash has raised $2.5B and is the largest US meal-delivery company.

Big things start small.

After an IPO on December 9th, 2020 DoorDash (DASH) has a market cap of $56B as of December 13, 2020.

Source: CNBC
Published: December 2019

January 10, 2020

The Story of Instant Pot

The Instant Pot is a programmable pressure and multi cooker. It speeds up cooking by up to 10 times using 70% less energy.

2009: Robert Wang (Computer Science Ph.D) founds Instant Brands. Wang self-funds the research and development of the first product investing $300,000 over 18 months.

2010: The Instant Pot makes its first sale on the Amazon Marketplace for $140.

2011: Wang reads every single customer review on Amazon. He uses them to continuously iterate on the product.

2017: Wang reads 40,000 reviews to date and can't keep up with reading each new review.

2018: During Prime Day, more than 300,000 Instant Pots are bought on Amazon.

2019: Corelle (owner of brands such as Pyrex) merges with Instant Brands for a market value of $2B.

2020: The Instant Pot Facebook group reaches 2.3M members who share and discuss recipes.

Source: CNBC
Published: December 2019

The Story of Instant Pot

The Instant Pot is a programmable pressure & multi cooker. It speeds up cooking by up to 10 times using up to 70% less energy.

- **2009:** Robert Wang (Computer Science Ph.D.) founds Instant Brands. Wang self-funds the research and development of the first product investing $300k over 18 months.
- **2010:** The Instant Pot makes its first sale on the Amazon Marketplace for $140.
- **2011:** Wang reads every single customer review on Amazon. He uses them to continuously iterate on the product.
- **2017:** Wang reads 40,000 reviews to date and can't keep up with reading each new review.
- **2018:** During Prime Day, more than 300,000 Instant Pots are bought on Amazon.
- **2019:** Corelle (owner of brands such as Pyrex) merges with Instant Brands for a market value of $2 billion.
- **2020:** The Instant Pot Facebook group reaches 2.3 million members who share and discuss recipes.

"Instant Pot is a remarkable business story. Innovation can open up forgotten market opportunity."

— **Chetan Puttagunta, Benchmark**

Source: Business Insider

Published: July 2015

March 26, 2020

From magnetrons to the microwave

In 1945, Percy Spencer was working in a lab testing magnetrons, the high-powered vacuum tubes inside radars. One day while working near the magnetrons that produced microwaves, Spencer noticed a peanut butter candy bar in his pocket had begun to melt — shortly after, the microwave oven was born.

With his newfound knowledge on how to cook food in mere seconds, Spencer and his employer, Raytheon, patented the invention. Two years later, they launched the first commercial microwave oven, which cost $5,000 at the time ($60,000 today) and weighed 750 pounds (340 kg).

By 1986 25% of American households owned a microwave, which rose to 90% in 1997, and 96% in 2012.

Source: Business Insider
Published: July 2015

From Magnetrons to the Microwave

In 1945, Percy Spencer was working in a lab testing magnetrons, the high-powered vacuum tubes inside radars. One day while working near the magnetrons that produced microwaves, Spencer noticed a peanut butter candy bar in his pocket had begun to melt — shortly after, the microwave oven was born.

With his newfound knowledge on how to cook food in mere seconds, Spencer and his employer, Raytheon, patented the invention. Two years later, they launched the first commercial microwave oven, which cost $5,000 at the time ($60,000 today) and weighed 750 pounds (340 kg).

By 1986, 25% of American households owned a microwave, which rose to 90% in 1997, and 96% in 2012.

Source: The Hustle
Published: November 2017

How a janitor at Frito-Lay invented Flamin' Hot Cheetos

In the mid-1980s PepsiCo CEO Roger Enrico recorded a video message for the company's 300k employees encouraging "acting like an owner." One night, a janitor Richard Montañez scooped up some Cheetos that hadn't yet been dusted in cheese, took them home and (with his wife) covered them in chili powder and "secret" spices.

Montañez called Enrico (the number was in the company directory) to tell the CEO he'd heeded the call to action. He'd studied the company's products, identified demand in the market, and crafted his own rudimentary snack in his kitchen. Enrico loved the ingenuity and asked Montañez to prepare a presentation for his executive team.

Six months later, Frito-Lay — a PepsiCo company — began testing Flamin' Hot Cheetos in Latino markets in East Los Angeles. In 1992, Flamin' Hot Cheetos was greenlit for a national release. The snack quickly became one of the most successful product launches in Frito-Lay history.

"Don't take your position for granted, regardless of what your position may be. CEO or janitor, act like you own the company."

— Montañez, VP of Multicultural Sales and Community Promotions at PepsiCo

Source: The Hustle
Published: November 2017

How a Janitor at Frito-Lay Invented Flamin' Hot Cheetos

In the mid-1980s, PepsiCo CEO Roger Enrico recorded a video message for the company's 300k employees encouraging *"acting like an owner"*. One night, Richard Montañez — a janitor at Frito-Lay- scooped up some Cheetos that hadn't yet been dusted in cheese, took them home and (with his wife) covered them in chili powder and "secret" spices.

Montañez called Enrico (the number was in the company directory) to tell him he'd heeded the call to action. He'd studied the company's products, identified a demand in the market, and crafted his own rudimentary snack in his kitchen. Enrico loved the ingenuity and asked Montañez to prepare a presentation for his executive team.

Six months later, Frito-Lay began testing Flamin' Hot Cheetos in Latino markets in East Los Angeles. In 1992, Flamin' Hot Cheetos were greenlit for a national release. The snack quickly became one of the most successful product launches in Frito-Lay history.

"Don't take your position for granted, regardless of what that position may be. CEO or janitor, act like you own the company."

— Richard Montañez, VP of Multicultural Sales & Community Promotions at PepsiCo

Source: Assorted
Published: August 2019

Fashion Tech Innovators

The RealReal

A marketplace for authenticated luxury consignment
"We take off of the top of eBay and the bottom off Sotheby's." — CEO Julie Wainwright
2018 revenue: $184M

Poshmark

Peer-to-peer marketplace focused on social commerce
"To be honest, the scale and the speed of resale-based commerce has caught me by surprise." — CEO Manish Chandra

2018 revenue estimate: $150M

Revolve

Millenial-focused marketplace with private brands
"We are more targeted than department stores with a greater selection than specialty retailers." — CEO Michael Mente
2018 revenue: $499M

ThredUp

Online thrift store for high-quality secondhand clothes
"Mass market or luxury, if people can find a high-quality product for much less, they'll choose used." — CEO James Reinhart
2018 revenue estimate: $38M

Source: Assorted
Published: August 2019

Fashion Tech Innovators

TheRealReal

- A marketplace for authenticated luxury consignment.
- "We take off of the top of eBay and the bottom off Sotheby's."
  — CEO Julie Wainwright
- 2018 revenue: $184M

Poshmark

- Peer-to-peer marketplace focused on social commerce.
- "To be honest, the scale and the speed of resale-based commerce has caught me by surprise."
  — CEO Manish Chandra
- 2018 revenue estimate: $150M

Revolve

- Millennial-focused marketplace with private brands.
- "We are more targeted than department stores with a greater selection than specialty retailers."
  — CEO Michael Mente
- 2018 revenue: $499M

ThredUp

- Online thrift store for high-quality secondhand clothes.
- "Mass market or luxury, if people can find a high-quality product for much less, they'll choose used."
  — CEO James Reinhart
- 2018 revenue estimate: $38M

Source: Harvard Business Review   January 9, 2020
Published: August 2018

The age of startup founders

Researchers looked at U.S. Census Bureau data to identify the average age of a successful startup founder.

- Entrepreneurs average age is 42.
    (e.g., dry cleaners and restaurants)

- Software startup founder is 40.

- Biotechnology founder is 47.

- The top 0.1% based on first five year growth is 45.

Takeaway:

Work experience plays a critical role in starting a successful company. Relative to founders with no relevant experience, those with at least 3 years of prior work experience in the same narrow industry as their startup were 85% more likely to launch a highly successful startup. Bill Gates, Steve Jobs, and Mark Zuckerberg truly are outliers.

Source: Harvard Business Review
Published: August 2018

The Age of Startup Founders

Researchers looked at U.S. Census Bureau data to identify the average age of a successful startup founder.

- Entrepreneurs average age is 42 (e.g., dry cleaners and restaurants).
- Software startup founder is 40.
- Biotechnology founder is 47.
- The top *0.1%* based on first five year growth is 45.

Work experience plays a critical role in starting a successful company. Relative to founders with no relevant experience, those with at least three years of prior work experience in the same narrow industry as their startup were *85%* more likely to launch a highly successful startup. Bill Gates, Steve Jobs, and Mark Zuckerberg truly are outliers.

Source: Starbucks

Published: November 2018

Why Starbucks loves gift cards

Gift card balances function as a loan to companies, such as Starbucks.

Starbucks does not pay interest on balances held in the Starbucks app or on gift cards.

As of September 2018, Starbucks customers held $1.63 billion of gift card balances. When a card experiences "long periods of inactivity" Starbucks recognizes this as breakage income.

Customers are forgetful and can lose cards leading to $155.9 million of breakage income in fiscal 2018, or 9.6% of gift card balances.

Source: Starbucks
Published: November 2018

Why Starbucks loves gift cards

Gift card balances function as a loan to companies, such as Starbucks. Starbucks does not pay interest on balances held in the Starbucks app or on gift cards.

As of September 2018, Starbucks customers held *$1.63 billion* of gift card balances. When a card experiences *"long periods of inactivity"*, Starbucks recognizes this as breakage income. Customers are forgetful and can lose cards leading to *$155.9 million* of breakage income in fiscal 2018, or *9.6%* of gift card balances.

Source: Netflix

Published: May 2020

May 27, 2020

Netflix helping members

You know that sinking feeling when you realize you signed up for something but haven't used it in ages? In a blog post, Netflix shared that the last thing they want is for people paying for something they're not using.

Netflix is now asking everyone who has not watched anything for a year since they joined to confirm they want to keep their membership. If customers don't confirm they want to keep subscribing, Netflix is automatically canceling their subscriptions.

"We hope this new approach saves people some hard earned cash."

— Eddy Wu, Product Innovation at Netflix

Source: Netflix
Published: May 2020

Netflix Helping Members

You know that sinking feeling when you realize you signed up for something but haven't used it in ages? In a blog post, Netflix shared that the last thing they want is for people paying for something they're not using.

Netflix is now asking everyone who has not watched anything for a year since they joined to confirm they want to keep their membership. If customers don't confirm they want to keep subscribing, Netflix is automatically canceling their subscription.

"We hope this new approach saves people some hard earned cash."

— Eddy Wu, Product Innovation at Netflix

Source: Google
Published: August 2020

Earthquake Detection on Your Phone

Android has recently partnered with world-renown seismologists to introduce the Android Earthquake Alerts System.

Smartphones house tiny accelerometers capable of detecting even the slightest movements. Android phones can serve as mini seismometers, and millions of Android phones linked together can serve as the world's largest earthquake detection network.

Aggregating this data can help to pinpoint an earthquake's epicenter, and provide immediate safety information to those in affected areas.

Source: Google
Published: August 2020

Earthquake Detection on Your Phone

Android has recently partnered with world-renown seismologists to introduce the Android Earthquake Alerts System.

Because smartphones house tiny accelerometers capable of detecting even the slightest movements, Android phones can serve as mini seismometers, and millions of Android phones linked together can serve as the world's largest earthquake detection network.

Aggregating this data can help to pinpoint an earthquake's epicenter, and provide immediate safety information to those in affected areas.

Source: IMDb

Published: October 2020

October 16, 2020

How answering a movie fan's question turned into IMDb

As with all good origin stories, IMDb had a humble beginning.

During the late 1980s, IMDb founder Col Needham was a member of an online discussion forum called rec.arts.movies, which was the place on the Internet to discuss movies.

In 1990, a member of the group was looking for a way to type the name of an actor/actress and generate a list of films in which they appeared.

Col Needham wrote a software program to solve the problem and shared it with the group, adding, "I am posting this message rather than mailing to give others the opportunity of experimenting with the script." In this spirit of collaboration, IMDb was born.

In 1998, Amazon made IMDb one of its first-ever acquisitions. With 200 million monthly visitors worldwide, it is now the world's most popular and authoritative source for information on movies, TV shows, and celebrities.

Source: IMDb
Published: October 2020

How answering a movie fan's question turned into IMDb

As with all good origin stories, IMDb had a humble beginning.

During the late 1980s, IMDb founder Col Needham was a member of an online discussion forum called rec.arts.movies, which was *the* place on the internet to discuss movies.

In 1990, a member of the group was looking for a way to type the name of an actor/actress and generate a list of films in which they appeared.

Col Needham wrote a software program to solve the problem and shared it with the group, adding, *"I am posting this message rather than mailing to give others the opportunity of experimenting with the script."* In this spirit of collaboration, IMDb was born.

In 1998, Amazon made IMDb one of its first-ever acquisitions. With 200 million monthly visitors worldwide, it is now the world's most popular and authoritative source for information on movies, TV shows, and celebrities.

Bonus: Col keeps track of every movie he's seen, totaling 12,600+ movies (not counting replays), and he watches an average of two films per day.

Source: Col Needham
Published: October 2020

A response to How answering a movie fan's question turned into IMDb

To all of the *Fact of the Day 1* readers,

First, thanks to Danny for allowing me to do a little follow-up here.

The past 30 years with IMDb have surpassed my wildest expectations. Thanks to our customers, team members, and passionate fan base, I get to spend my time building and working with some of the most creative people in the world.

We also owe a debt of thanks to Will Smith.

In 1996, we needed to buy our first server. It was time to move on from borrowed capacity at colleges around the world. We put the server purchase on a personal credit card. Before the bill was due, we managed to sell our first piece of advertising for three times the cost of the server, helping IMDb to (accidentally) become one of the first profitable web sites. A few months later, we sold our first movie ad campaign to Twentieth Century Fox for *Independence Day* which was my cue to quit my day job and become IMDb's first paid employee. Will Smith was amused when I had the opportunity to relate this story to him at The Cannes Film Festival some 21 years later.

In 1998, when we first sat down to talk about a possible acquisition with Jeff Bezos, we wanted to understand how IMDb would fit within the larger Amazon company. Jeff explained how IMDb could retain our web site and brand, where the information would continue to be optimized for search, browse, and contribution, while Amazon.com would build the world's best video store using IMDb's information -- and that's exactly what happened.

Today, IMDb content is integrated into some of Amazon's most-loved devices and services, including Amazon Fire TV, Alexa, and X-Ray on Prime Video.

Looking for a movie recommendation? I've watched a few in my time, as Danny mentioned. I made an IMDb list, naturally, of my favourite movies from each of the last 30 years -- here are the three most recent:

- **The Shape of Water** (a much-deserved yet somewhat bold choice for Best Picture at The Oscars)
- **Wild Rose** (a wonderful film about pursuing your dreams)
- **Once Upon a Time... In Hollywood** (a fascinating look at what could have been)

"*All of life's riddles are answered in the movies,*" is a quote from the 1991 film *Grand Canyon*, and best sums up the power of film to entertain, educate, and change the world. If you do not believe this, then you simply have not yet seen enough movies!

Cheers,

Col

SECTION 2

HIRE AND DEVELOP THE BEST

CHAPTER 5

LEADERSHIP

Source: Jared Nielson
Published: Dec. 2018

March 29

Fixed Mindset	Growth Mindset
Believes that intelligence is static	Believes intelligence can be developed
avoids challenges	embraces challenges
get defensive or give up easily	persist regardless of setbacks
See effort as fruitless	See efforts as the path to mastery
ignore useful negative feedback	learn from criticism
feel threatened by the success of others	find lessons and inspiration from the success of others
desire to look smart	desire to learn

"Our industry does not respect tradition. What it respects is innovation.

Culture eats strategy for breakfast."

— Satya Nadella, CEO Microsoft

Source: Jared Nielsen
Published: December 2018

Fixed Mindset vs Growth Mindset

Fixed Mindset	Growth Mindset
Believes that intelligence is static...	*Believes intelligence can be developed...*
...avoids challenges	...embrace challenges
...get defensive or give up easily	...persist in the face of setbacks
...see effort as fruitless	...see efforts as the path to mastery
...ignore useful negative feedback	...learn from criticism
...feel threatened by the success of others	...find lessons and inspiration in the success of others
...which leads to a desire to look smart and therefore a tendency to...	...which leads to a desire to learn and therefore a tendency to...

"Our industry does not respect tradition. What it respects is innovation. Culture eats strategy for breakfast."

—**Satya Nadella, CEO Microsoft**

Source: Google
Published: February 2018

What makes a manager great

In 2008 a team of Google researchers launched Project Oxygen – an effort to determine what makes a manager great. They learned that eight behaviors are common among the highest performing managers.
In 2018, this list expanded to ten.

The 10 behaviors of Google's best managers

- Is a good coach
- Empowers team and does not micromanage
- Creates an inclusive team environment, showing concern for success and well-being
- Is productive and results-oriented
- Is a good communicator – listens and shares information
- Supports career development and discusses performance
- Has a clear vision/strategy for the team
- Has key technical skills to help advise the team
- Collaborates across the company
- Is a strong decision maker

Source: Google
Published: February 2018

What Makes a Manager Great

In 2008, a team of Google researchers launched Project Oxygen — an effort to determine what makes a manager great. They learned that eight behaviors are common among the highest performing managers. In 2018, this list expanded to ten.

Note: While Google uncovered what makes a great manager at the company, it doesn't mean what works for Google managers will work for any organization.

The 10 behaviors of Google's best managers:

- Is a good coach.
- Empowers team and does not micromanage.
- Creates an inclusive team environment, showing concern for success and well-being.
- Is productive and results-oriented.
- Is a good communicator — listens and shares information.
- Supports career development and discusses performance.
- Has a clear vision/strategy for the team.
- Has key technical skills to help advise the team.
- Collaborates across the company.
- Is a strong decision maker.

Source: Radical Candor
Published: March 2017

Radical Candor

Author Kim Scott was an executive at Google and then at Apple, where she worked with a team to develop a class on how to be a good manager.

Radical candor is the idea that to be a good boss, you have to care personally at the same time that you challenge directly.

This framework can help you build better relationships at work and fulfill your three key responsibilities as a leader:

1. creating a culture of feedback
   (praise and criticism)
2. building a cohesive team
3. achieving results you're all proud of

Care personally / challenge directly quadrant:
- Ruinous Empathy
- RADICAL CANDOR ✓
- Manipulative Insincerity
- Obnoxious Aggression
- silence
- Challenge directly
- rage

Source: Radical Candor
Published: March 2017

Radical Candor

Author Kim Scott was an executive at Google and then at Apple, where she worked with a team to develop a class on how to be a good manager. Radical candor is the idea that to be a good boss, you have to care personally at the same time that you challenge directly.

This framework can help you build better relationships at work and fulfill your three key responsibilities as a leader:

1. creating a culture of feedback (praise and criticism)
2. building a cohesive team
3. achieving results you're all proud of

Radical candor: When you care personally and challenge directly.

Ruinous empathy: When you care, but don't challenge.

Manipulative insincerity: When neither care, nor challenge

Obnoxious aggression: When you challenge, but don't care about how your words are received.

Source: Harvard Business Review
Published: August 2019

May 18, 2020

The sponsorship spectrum

Sponsorship is a kind of helping relationship in which senior, powerful people use their clout to talk up, advocate for, and place a more junior person in a key role. While a mentor is someone who has knowledge and will share it with you, a sponsor is a person who has power, and will use it for you.

Private relationship ↑

① Mentor: provide advice, support, or coaching

② Strategizer: share insider information about advancing; strategize getting ahead

③ Connector: make introductions to influential people; talk them up with your peers

④ Opportunity giver: provide a high-visibility opportunity

⑤ Advocate: publicly advocate a promotion; fight for them in settings where they can't fight for themself

Public relationship ↓

Source: Harvard Business Review
Published: August 2019

The Sponsorship Spectrum

Sponsorship is a kind of helping relationship in which senior, powerful people use their clout to talk up, advocate for, and place a more junior person in a key role. While a mentor is someone who has knowledge and will share it with you, a sponsor is a person who has power and will use it for you.

The spectrum starts with private relationships and ends with public relationships.

1. Mentor: provide advice, support, or coaching
2. Strategizer: share insider information about advancing; strategize getting ahead
3. Connector: make introductions to influential people; talk them up with your peers
4. Opportunity giver: provide a high-visibility opportunity
5. Advocate: publicly advocate a promotion; fight for them in settings when they can't fight for themself

Source: Bush Center   October 9, 2020
Published: April 2018

Leadership Style as a Company Scales

Question:

How has your leadership style changed over the years?

Answer by Jeff Bezos:

When the company is 10 or 100 people, I can be involved in every decision, not just the objectives like 'what are we going to do?' but the methods like 'how are we going to do it?'

As a company gets bigger, the CEO or founder cannot be involved in all of those decisions - certainly not in the methods of how things get done. You surely need to change your leadership style as the company scales.

The principles of the company have not changed, I spend more of my time on culture and setting high standards such as customer obsession and inventiveness.

I am kind of a teacher now!

Source: Bush Center
Published: April 2018

Leadership Style as a Company Scales

Question:

"How has your leadership style changed over the years?"

Answer by Jeff Bezos:

"When the company is 10 or 100 people, I can be involved in every decision, not just the objectives like *'what are we going to do?'* but the methods like *'how are we going to do it?'*

As a company gets bigger, the CEO or founder cannot be involved in all of those decisions — certainly not in the methods of *how* things get done. You surely need to change your leadership style as the company scales.

The principles of the company have not changed. I spend more of my time on culture and setting high standards such as customer obsession and inventiveness.

I am kind of a teacher now!"

Source: Harvard Business Review   September 27

Published: June 2019

n= 3,973 people in corporate talent-acquisition

Channels for new hires

Employers spend an enormous amount on hiring - on average $4,129 per job in the United States. The most popular channel for finding new hires is through employee referrals.

	Respondents
Employee referrals	48%
Third-party websites or online job boards	46
Social or professional networks	40
Third-party recruiters or staffing firms	34
Internal hires	28

Note: based on a 2017 survey from LinkedIn where respondents selected the top channels for quality hires

Source: Harvard Business Review
Published: June 2019
n = 3,973 people in corporate talent-acquisition

Channels for New Hires

Employers spend an enormous amount on hiring — an average of *$4,129 per job* in the United States. The most popular channel for finding new hires is through employee referrals.

Channel	Respondents
Employee referrals	48%
Third-party websites or online job boards	46%
Social or professional networks	40%
Third-party recruiters or staffing firms	34%
Internal hires	28%

CHAPTER 6

DIVERSITY & INCLUSION

Source: William H. Frey's Analysis of U.S. Census
Published: March 2019

April 3

Racial profile of U.S. population, 2045

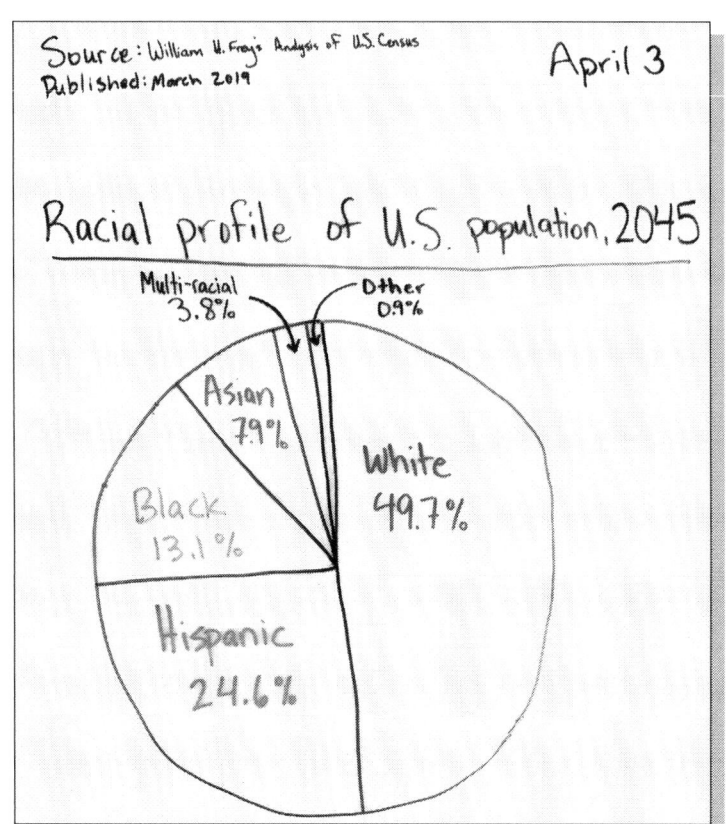

Multi-racial
3.8%

Other
0.9%

Asian
7.9%

Black
13.1%

White
49.7%

Hispanic
24.6%

Source: William H. Frey's analysis of U.S. Census
Published: March 2019

Racial Profile of the US Population in 2045

- **White** — 49.7%
- **Hispanic** — 24.6%
- **Black** — 13.1%
- **Asian** — 7.9%
- **Multi-racial** — 3.8%
- **Other** — 0.9%

Source: Hannah Arendt   June 8, 2020

Published: August 1987

Submitted by: Black Employee Network (BEN)

<u>Collective guilt vs. Collective responsibility</u>

Collective guilt

- Definition: the idea that the individuals in a group are guilty of the harm caused by the other individuals in the group.

- Can be harmful and distract or hinder action.

- How does it look?
  ↳ Individuals expressing guilt or shame or apologizing profusely on behalf of their offending group.

Collective responsibility

- Definition: the idea that the individuals in a group are responsible to fix the harm caused by other individuals in the group.

- Can be empowering and conducive to action.

- How does it look?
  ↳ Individuals spreading awareness of the problem and ways to act to fix it and taking concrete actions to do so.

Source: Hannah Arendt
Published: August 1987
Submitted by: Amazon's Black Employee Network (BEN)

Collective Guilt vs. Collective Responsibility

	Collective guilt	Collective responsibility
Definition	The idea that the individuals in a group are guilty of the harm caused by the other individuals in the group.	The idea that the individuals in a group are responsible to fix the harm caused by other individuals in the group.
Description	Can be harmful and distract from or hinder action.	Can be beneficial and is empowering and conducive to action.
How does it look?	Individuals expressing guilt or shame or apologizing profusely on behalf of their offending group.	Individuals spreading awareness of the problem and ways to act to fix it and taking concrete actions to do so.

Source: Design in Tech
Published: March 2019

June 4, 2020

<u>Illustrations addressing imbalance</u>

The 2019 "Design in Tech" report (published by John Maeda, Chief Experience Officer at Publicis Sapient) featured visualizations of:

Inequality: unequal access to opportunities

Equality: evenly distributed tools and assistance

Equity: custom tools that identify and address inequality

Justice: fixing the system to offer equal access to both tools and opportunities

See the attached images that are outside my artistic ability.

Source: Design in Tech
Published: March 2019

Illustrations Addressing Imbalance

The 2019 Design in Tech report (published by John Maeda, Chief Experience Officer at Publicis Sapient) featured visualizations of:

Inequality: unequal access to opportunities

Equality: evenly distributed tools and assistance

Equity: custom tools that identify and address inequality

Justice: fixing the system to offer equal access to both tools and opportunities

Illustrations inspired by *The Giving Tree*. Images: 2019 Design in Tech Report

Source: Black Employee Network (BEN)
Submitted by: Anthony Cole and Angelina Howard

Amazon's First Affinity Group

In August 2005 Gino White stood up at an
All Hands and asked Jeff Bezos:

"Why doesn't Amazon have an affinity group
for Black employees?"

Jeff responded:

"You should start one!"

Gino accepted the challenge and started BEN,
Amazon's first affinity group. BEN

has grown to 2,000+ Amazonians across
the world. BEN's purpose is to:

provide a support structure for Black
employees at Amazon and to champion
diversity throughout the company.

Source: Amazon's Black Employee Network (BEN)
Published: April 2019

Amazon's First Affinity Group

In August 2005, Gino White stood up at All Hands and asked Jeff Bezos, *"Why doesn't Amazon have an affinity group for Black employees?"*

Jeff's answer: *"You should start one!"*

Gino accepted the challenge and created the Black Employee Network, Amazon's first affinity group. BEN has grown to include thousands of Amazonians across the world to provide a support structure for Black employees at Amazon and champion diversity throughout the company.

Source: AI Now Institute, NYU

Published: April 2019

June 25

Diversity in the Artificial Intelligence Industry

- Women comprise 15% of AI research staff at Facebook and 10% at Google

- At leading AI conferences, 18% of speakers are women

- 80% of AI professors are male

- 2.5% of Google's workforce is black, Facebook and Microsoft are each at 4%.

Source: AI Now Institute, NYU
Published: April 2019

Diversity in the Artificial Intelligence Industry

- Women comprise *15%* of AI research staff at Facebook and *10%* at Google.
- At leading AI conferences, *18%* of speakers are women.
- *80%* of AI professors are male.
- *2.5%* of Google's workforce is black, Facebook and Microsoft are each at *4%*.

Source: Center for Disease Control
Published: August 2018

The prevalence of disabilities

25.7% of non-institutionalized U.S. adults (61 million people) report at least one disability. With age, disability becomes more common, affecting about 2 in 5 adults age 65+.

Disability	Description	% of Adults
Mobility	serious difficulty walking or climbing stairs	13.7%
Cognition	serious difficulty concentrating, remembering, or making decisions	10.8%
Hearing	serious difficulty hearing	6.8%
Vision	serious difficulty seeing	5.9%
Independent Living	difficulty doing errands alone	4.6%
Self-Care	difficulty dressing or bathing	3.7%

October is National Disability Employment Awareness Month.

Source: Center for Disease Control
Published: August 2018

The Prevalence of Disabilities

25.7% of non-institutionalized U.S. adults (*61 million people*) report at least one disability. With age, disability becomes more common, affecting about *2 in 5 adults age 65+*.

Disability	Description	% of Adults
Mobility	serious difficulty walking or climbing stairs	13.7%
Cognition	serious difficulty concentrating, remembering, or making decisions	10.8%
Hearing	serious difficulty hearing	6.8%
Vision	serious difficulty seeing	5.9%
Independent living	difficulty doing errands alone	4.6%
Self-care	difficulty dressing or bathing	3.7%

Building Products for People with Disabilities

In the U.S. nearly 40MM people over the age of 15 self-identify as having a disability, representing 12.6% of the non-institutionalized population. Globally, an estimated 785MM (15%) to 975MM (19%) of people live with a disability - representing difficulties with:

- hearing
- vision
- cognition
- mobility

Combined, people with disabilities control $8 trillion in annual disposable income.

Source: World Health Organization
Published: July 2011

Building Products for People with Disabilities

In the US, nearly 40M people over the age of 15 self-identify as having a disability, representing 12.6% of the non-institutionalized population. Globally, an estimated 785M (15%) to 975M (19%) people over the age of 15 live with a disability — representing people with disabilities across difficulties with hearing, vision, cognition and/or mobility. Combined, people with a disability (PWD) control $8 trillion in annual disposable income.

Source: ResumeGo
Published: February 2019
Submitted by: Black Employee Network (BEN)

Whitened resumes

Background

Resume whitening is the practice of job applicants from underrepresented groups removing references to their race on their resumes in the hope of increasing their chance of getting an interview.

Field Experiment

ResumeGo submitted 19,200 fictitious resumes on job search websites such as Indeed, CareerBuilder, and ZipRecruiter. Resumes were submitted with Black-sounding names, Asian-sounding names, and White-sounding names and callback rates were recorded and compared.

Findings

White applicants received 55% more callbacks than Black applicants and 31% more callbacks than Asian applicants. Applicants faced the least racial descrimination when applying to jobs in Technology and the most for jobs in Finance.

Source: ResumeGo
Published: February 2019
Submitted by: Amazon Black Employee Network (BEN)

Whitened Resumes

Background

"Resume whitening" is the practice of job applicants from underrepresented groups removing references to their race on their resumes in the hope of increasing their chance of getting an interview.

Field Experiment

ResumeGo submitted 19,200 fictitious resumes on job search websites such as Indeed, CareerBuilder, and ZipRecruiter. Resumes were submitted with Black-sounding names, Asian-sounding names, and White-sounding names and callback rates were recorded and compared.

Findings

White applicants received 55% more callbacks than Black applicants and 31% more callbacks than Asian applicants. Applicants faced the least racial discrimination when applying to jobs in Technology and the most for jobs in Finance.

Source: Amazon, Apple, Facebook, Google, Microsoft, Netflix, US Census
Published: Assorted
Submitted by: Black Employee Network (BEN)

June 11, 2020

Diversity in Tech

Representation matters.

Diversity and Inclusion reports allow us to compare the percentage of Black representation in tech companies to the US baseline.

Amazon shares data on managers, separate from the overall employee population.

Organization	Date Published	Black/African American representation of US employees
US Census Bureau	July 2019	13%
Amazon all employees	December 2019	27%
Amazon managers	December 2019	8%
Apple	December 2018	9%
Facebook	July 2019	4%
Google	May 2020	4%
Microsoft	November 2019	4%
Netflix	April 2020	7%

Source: Amazon, Apple, Facebook, Google, Microsoft, Netflix, US Census
Published: Assorted
Submitted by: Amazon Black Employee Network (BEN)

Diversity in Tech

Representation matters. Diversity and Inclusion reports allow us to compare the percentage of Black representation in tech companies to the US baseline. Amazon shares data on managers, separate from the overall employee population.

Note that Amazon's figure includes operations (ranging from fulfillment centers to data centers) along with corporate jobs.

Organization	Date Published	Black/African American representation of US employees
US Census Bureau	July 2019	13%
Amazon All Employees	December 2019	27%
Amazon Mangers	December 2019	8%
Apple	December 2018	9%
Facebook	July 2019	4%
Google	May 2020	4%
Microsoft	November 2019	4%
Netflix	April 2020	7%

CHAPTER 7

PRODUCT
DEVELOPMENT

Source: Agile Alliance
Published: February 2001

Agile Manifesto

In Snowbird, Utah, in 2001, 17 people met to discuss the future of software development. The Agile Manifesto, a 68-word document emerged. It reads:

We are uncovering better ways of developing software by doing it and helping others do it. Through this, we have come to value:

- Individuals and interactions over processes and tools

- Working software over comprehensive documentation

- Customer collaboration over contract negotiation

- Responding to change over following a plan

Source: Agile Alliance
Published: February 2001

Agile Manifesto

In Snowbird, Utah, in 2001, 17 people met to discuss the future of software development. The Agile Manifesto, a 68-word document, emerged. It reads:

We are uncovering better ways of developing software by doing it and helping others do it. Through this work, we have come to value:

- **Individuals and interactions** over processes and tools
- **Working software** over comprehensive documentation
- **Customer collaboration** over contract negotiation
- **Responding to change** over following a plan

Source: Martin Fowler
Published: May 2019

Technical debt

During the planning or execution of a software project, leaders make decisions to defer necessary work.

For example, one might say,

"we're not following the company's User Interface guidelines, but we'll get to it in the next version."

Technical debt is a software engineering metaphor to explain this type of trade-off. As you take on more tech debt, you get faster deployments but your system becomes harder to modify in the future.

Leaders can, therefore:

1) Keep an explicit tech debt list and share it with your team (and partner teams)

2) Note the consequences of each item

3) Allow time on the schedule to "pay off" the debt by making the code clearer and simpler without creating new functionality (i.e., refactoring)

Source: Martin Fowler
Published: May 2019

Technical Debt

During the planning or execution of a software project, leaders make decisions to defer necessary work. For example, one might say, *"we're not following the company's User Interface guidelines, but we'll get to it in the next version."*

Technical debt is a software development metaphor to explain this type of trade-off. As you take on more tech debt, you get faster deployments, but your system becomes harder to modify in the future.

Leaders can, therefore:

1. Keep an explicit tech debt list and share it with your team (and partner teams)
2. Note the consequences of each item
3. Allow time on the schedule to "pay off" the debt by making the code clearer and simpler without creating new functionality (i.e., refactoring)

Source: Shreyas Doshi
Published: September 2020

December 2, 2020

A Product Metrics Primer

When building software, product owners need to decide which behaviors and uses are the most important to measure. The following categories can help you choose the metrics for your software products that matter most to your customers and your business.

Metric	Description	Examples
Health	Is the product performing reliably?	latency, initial load time, uptime
Usage	How are customers using the product?	day of week trends, help documentation visits, visits by country
Adoption	Are consumers using the product as much as we'd hope, and in the ways that we'd like?	monthly active users, free-to-paid conversions, new features
Satisfaction	What is our customers' overall sentiment towards the product?	net promoter score, customer satisfaction score
Ecosystem	How does the product compare with substitute offerings from competitors?	share of wallet, third party integrations, industry rank
Outcome	What overall results are we seeing from this product?	revenue per user, gross margin, transactions

Source: Shreyas Doshi
Published: September 2020

A Product Metrics Primer

When building software, product owners need to decide which behaviors and uses are the most important to measure.

The following categories can help you choose the metrics for your software products that matter most to your customers and your business.

Metric	Description	Examples
Health	Is the product performing reliably?	latency, initial load time, uptime
Usage	How are customers using the product?	day-of-week trends, help documentation visits, visits by country
Adoption	Are consumers using the product as much as we'd hope, and in the ways that we'd like?	monthly active users, free-to-paid conversions, new features
Satisfaction	What is our customers' overall sentiment towards the product?	net promoter score, customer satisfaction score
Ecosystem	How does the product compare with substitute offerings from competitors?	share of wallet, third party integrations, industry rank
Outcome	What overall results are we seeing from this product?	revenue per user, gross margin, transactions

Benefits versus Features

Benefits help the customer understand how your product or service will improve their life.

Features enable the benefits, but they're usually not what motivates customers to act.

Non-technical Example: Whole-grain bread

Benefit 25 grams of whole-grains per day reduces the risk of heart disease by 15%.

Feature Contains whole-grains.

Technical Example: Amazon Aurora (relational database)

Benefit performance of commercial databases at $1/10^{th}$ the cost.

Feature auto-scales up to 64TB per database instance.

Source: *Fact of the Day 1*
Published: December 2019

Benefits versus Features

Benefits help the customer understand how your product or service will improve their life.

Features enables the benefit, but they're usually not what motivates customers to act.

Non-technical example: **whole-grain bread.**

- **Benefit** — 25 grams of whole-grains per day reduces the risk of heart disease by 15% (WebMD).
- **Feature** — contains whole-grains.

Technical example: **Amazon Aurora (relational database).**

- **Benefit** — performance of commercial databases at 1/10th the cost (AWS).
- **Feature** — auto-scales up to 64TB per database instance.

Source: Project Smart   October 22, 2020
Published: May 2014

The MoSCoW Method

There is always more to do than time or funding permits, hence the need for prioritization.

The MoSCoW method is a prioritization technique used in management, business analysis, project management, and software development to reach a common understanding with stakeholders on the importance they place on the delivery of each requirement.

M - MUST meet this requirement to be viable, non-negotiable.

S - SHOULD meet this requirement to achieve success, important but not vital.

C - COULD meet this requirement if efficient, a nice to have.

W - WOULD like to provide this requirement in the future; re-evaluate later.

Example: Customer requirements for autonomous vehicles may be categorized as

M- MUST be safe and reliable.

S- SHOULD be more fuel-efficient than vehicles today.

C - COULD be more spacious without a need for the steering wheel.

W- WOULD be nice if it parked itself after dropping a rider off.

Source: Project Smart
Published: May 2014

The MoSCoW Method

There is always more to do than time or funding permits, hence the need for prioritization.

The MoSCoW method is a prioritization technique used in management, business analysis, project management, and software development to reach a common understanding with stakeholders on the importance they place on the delivery of each requirement.

M - MUST meet this requirement to be viable, non-negotiable.

S - SHOULD meet this requirement to achieve success, important but not vital.

C - COULD meet this requirement if efficient, a nice to have.

W - WOULD like to provide this requirement in the future; re-evaluate later.

Example: Customer requirements for autonomous vehicles may be categorized as

M - MUST be safe and reliable.

S - SHOULD be more fuel-efficient than vehicles today.

C - COULD be more spacious without a need for the steering wheel.

W - WOULD be nice if it parked itself after dropping a rider off.

Source: User Interviews
Published: February 2020
n= 300 user researchers

March 16, 2020

User research methods

Qualitative research can be a rich source of customer anecdotes and big-picture insights that can inspire innovative thinking on behalf of customers. 96% of user researchers surveyed conduct more than one type of research study every month.

"Every anecdote from a customer matters. We research each of them because they tell us something about our processes. It's an audit that is done for us by our customers. We treat them as precious sources of information." — Jeff Wilke, CEO Worldwide Consumer

Type of study	Description	User researchers who use method
User interviews	One-on-one sessions to give insight into what users think and feel	92%
Moderated usability tests	the participant completes a task with a moderator as a guide	84
Surveys	gathering information by sampling the population	78
Field/Ethnographic Studies	observing participants perform a task in their own natural context	64
Unmoderated usability tests	the participant completes a task on their own	59
Card sorts	design information architecture of a site	54

Source: UserInterviews
Published: February 2020
n = 300 user researchers

User research methods

Qualitative research can be a rich source of customer anecdotes and big-picture insights that can inspire innovative thinking on behalf of customers. Researchers use a variety of methods to get the job done. 96% of user researchers surveyed conduct more than one type of research study every month.

"Every anecdote from a customer matters. We research each of them because they tell us something about our processes. It's an audit that is done for us by our customers. We treat them as precious sources of information"

—Jeff Wilke, CEO Worldwide Consumer at Amazon

Type of Studies	Description	% of Researchers
User interviews	One-on-one sessions to give insight into what users think and feel	92%
Moderated usability tests	The participant completes a task with a moderator as a guide	84%
Surveys	Gathering information by sampling the population	78%
Field/Ethnographic studies	Observing participants perform a task in their own natural context	64%
Unmoderated usability tests	The participant completes a task on their own	59%
Card sorts	Design information architecture of a site	54%
First click tests	Examine how users get around the site	36%
Accessibility tests	Ensure usability by people with disabilities (e.g., hearing, color blindness)	36%
Diary studies	Learn about behaviors over time	31%
Tree tests	Evaluate the findability of topics in a website	27%

Source: Smashing Magazine   November 10, 2020
Published: June 2020

Improving User Interview Questions

A user interview is a UX research method during which a researcher asks one user questions about a topic of interest (e.g., a new feature) to learn about that topic. Unlike focus groups, user interviews are one-on-one sessions. Here are three ways to improve the questions you may ask:

Worse	Better	Learning
How probable is it that you use "Bookmarks"?	How can you use "Bookmarks"?	Avoid hypothetical questions.
Do you like this feature?	How has this feature helped you in your work?	Ask open ended questions
Do you check the "Daily Deals" daily or once a week?	How often do you check the "Daily Deals"?	Encourage the user to come up with their answer from scratch.

Source: Smashing Magazine
Published: June 2020

Improving User Interview Questions

A user interview is a UX research method during which a re-searcher asks one user questions about a topic of interest (e.g., a new feature) to learn about that topic. Unlike focus groups, user interviews are one-on-one sessions. Here are three ways to improve the questions you may ask:

Worse	Better	Learning
How probable is it that you use "Bookmarks"?	How can you use "Bookmarks"?	Avoid hypothetical questions.
Do you like this feature?	How has this feature helped you in your work?	Ask open-ended questions.
Do you check the "Daily Deals" daily or once a week?	How often do you check the "Daily Deals"?	Encourage the user to come up with their answer from scratch.

Source: Survey Monkey   September 4, 2020
Published: April 2019

Net Promoter Score

The Net Promoter Score (NPS) has long been a valuable and straightforward gauge for assessing a company's relationship with its customers. Customers are asked "On a scale of 0 to 10, how likely is it that you would recommend our product/service to a friend or colleague?"

"Promoters" are those customers who answer 9 or 10.

"Passively Satisfied" answer 7 or 8.

"Detractors" answer 0 to 6.

A NPS is calculated by the percentage of promoters minus the percentage of detractors. Scores range from -100 to +100. For example, a 35% promoter response less a 28% detractor response yields an NPS of +7 (35 - 28 = 7). NPS numbers provide the most significant benefit when measured over time, allowing you to recognize trends and address problems.

Source: Survey Monkey
Published: April 2019

Net Promoter Score

The Net Promoter Score (NPS) has long been a valuable and straightforward gauge for assessing a company's relationship with its customers. Customers are asked "On a scale of 0 to 10, how likely is it that you would recommend our product/service to a friend or colleague?"

"Promoters" are those customers who answer 9 or 10.

"Passively Satisfied" answer 7 or 8.

"Detractors" answer 0 to 6.

NPS is calculated by the percentage of promoters minus the percentage of detractors. Scores range from -100 to +100. For example, a *35% promoter* response less a *28% detractor* response yields an NPS of +7 (35–28 = 7). NPS numbers provide the most significant benefit when measured over time, allowing you to recognize trends and address problems.

Source: Modern Analyst
Published: November 2017

August 11, 2020

Cognitive load

Originating from the field of psychology, cognitive load refers to the amount of mental effort used in a person's working memory. (Think of RAM on a computer.) More cognitive load makes it more difficult for people to make decisions and complete tasks.

User experience (UX) designers can decrease the cognitive load by using standard icons such as drop-downs, toggles, sliders, and buttons. Heavy cognitive load has a direct and adverse effect on how well a user learns and uses a new application.

One way designers quantify cognitive load is by measuring pupil responses, allowing for detection of when a user's mind is being most taxed.

Source: Modern Analyst
Published: November 2017

Cognitive load

Originating from the field of psychology, cognitive load refers to the amount of mental effort used in a person's working memory — think of RAM on a computer. More cognitive load makes it more difficult for people to make decisions and complete tasks.

User experience (UX) designers can decrease the cognitive load by using standard icons such as drop-downs, toggles, sliders, and buttons. Heavy cognitive load has a direct and adverse effect on how well a user learns and uses a new application.

One way designers quantify cognitive load is by measuring pupil responses, allowing for detection of when a user's mind is being most taxed.

Source: Andreessen Horowitz   September 17, 2020
Published: April 2014

Ship It Before You Are Ready

A difficult decision in software development is determining when to make a new product or feature available to customers. Launching new functionality is referred to as "shipping it", originating in the era of floppy disks and CDs shipped in physical boxes.

Leaders have a hard time getting a product out the door. There's always more to do to get it right. The takeaway: "ship it", learn from customers, gather data, iterate, and repeat.

An example of a product shipped without full functionality is the original iPhone in 2007. It wasn't until the iPhone 3GS was released two years later that Apple 'shipped' a feature enabling users to Cut, Copy, and Paste.

Source: Andreessen Horowitz
Published: April 2014

Ship It Before You Are Ready

A difficult decision in software development is determining when to make a new product or feature available to customers. Launching new functionality is referred to as "*shipping it*," originating in the era of floppy disks and CDs shipped in physical boxes.

Leaders have a hard time getting a product out the door. There's always more to do to get it right. The takeaway: "*ship it*," learn from customers, gather data, iterate, and repeat.

An example of a product shipped without full functionality is the original iPhone in 2007. It wasn't until the iPhone 3GS was released two years later that Apple '*shipped*' a feature enabling users to Cut, Copy, and Paste.

Source: Nielsen Norman Group   June 22, 2020
Published: May 2020

Online information-seeking behaviors

User experience researchers identified three types of online information-seeking behaviors based on the user's purpose:

1. Acquire: The user looks for a fact, finds product information, or downloads something.

   Example: the steps to perform CPR

2. Compare/Choose: The user evaluates multiple products or information sources to make a decision.

   Example: Comparing the prices and features of Bluetooth headsets

3. Understand: The user gains an understanding of a topic.

   Example: deciding to mount your wifi router higher up on the wall for stronger signal throughout your home

Source: Nielsen Norman Group
Published: May 2020

Online Information-Seeking Behaviors

User experience researchers identified three types of online information-seeking behaviors based on the user's purpose:

1. **Acquire**: The user looks for a fact, finds product information, or downloads something.

    Example: the steps to perform CPR.

2. **Compare/Choose**: The user evaluates multiple products or information sources to make a decision.

    Example: comparing the prices and features of Bluetooth headsets.

3. **Understand**: The user gains an understanding of a topic.

    Example: deciding to mount your wifi router higher up on the wall for stronger signal throughout your home.

Source: Clay Christensen, Harvard Business Review
Published: September 2016

Jobs to be done theory

When we buy a product, we essentially hire it to help us do a job. If it does the job well, we'll hire it to help us do a job. If it does a crummy job, we fire it and look for something else to solve the problem.

The key to successful innovation is identifying jobs that are poorly performed in customers' lives and then designing products, experiences, and processes around those jobs.

Jobs to be done	Old solution	Amazon's innovative solution
Make a fresh dinner at home	Pick a recipe and grocery items	Amazon Meal Kit
Start reading a new book	Drive to bookstore	Download a Kindle e-book
Provision infrastructure resources in your cloud environment	Individually spin up resources and AWS services	AWS CloudFormation template with 'one-click' deployment
When not home, packages are stolen or mail delivery is missed	Drive to pick-up or re-order	Amazon Locker for self-service pick-up

Source: Clay Christensen, Harvard Business Review
Published: September 2016

Jobs to Be Done Theory

To create offerings that people truly want to buy, firms need to hone in on the job the customer is trying to get done. When we buy a product, we essentially "hire" it to help us do a job. If it does the job well, we'll hire it again. If it does a crummy job, we "fire" it and look for something else to solve the problem.

The key to successful innovation is identifying jobs that are poorly performed in customers' lives and then designing products, experiences, and processes around those jobs.

Jobs To Be Done	Old Solution	Amazon's Innovation Solution
Make a fresh dinner at home	Pick recipe & grocery items	Amazon Meal Kit
Start reading a new book	Drive to bookstore	Download a Kindle ebook
Provision infrastructure resources in your cloud environment	Individually spin up resources and AWS services	AWS CloudFormation template with 'one-click' deployment
When not home, packages are stolen or mail delivery is missing	Drive to pick-up or re-order	Amazon Locker for self-service pick-up

Source: Clockwork
Published: May 2020
Submitted by: Black Employee Network (BEN)

Inclusive naming conventions

Language is powerful. In our daily work and life, we may unconsciously encourage bias by using words and phrases that have historical context and implications of which we may not be aware.

Biased phrasing	Alternatives
Blacklist / Whitelist	AllowList / DenyList
Master / Slave	Primary / Replica Leader / Follower
Brown bags	Lunch and learn, Tech talks
Man hours	Hours of effort
Pow wow	Huddle, Standup, Discussion
Grandfathered	Legacy, exempt
"Hi Guys"	Y'all, folks
Black / Gray days	Blocked / Restricted days
Tribal knowledge	Institutional knowledge
Open the kimono	Full disclosure, Provide insight into

Source: Clockwork
Published: May 2020

Inclusive Naming Conventions

Language is powerful. In our daily work and life, we may unconsciously encourage bias by using words and phrases that have historical context and implications of which we may not be aware.

Biased Phrasing	Alternatives
Blacklist / Whitelist	AllowList / DenyList
Master / Slave	Primary / Replica, Leader / Follower
Man hours	Hours of effort
Pow wow	Huddle, Standup, Discussion
Grandfathered	Legacy, Exempt
Black / Gray days	Blocked / Restricted days
Tribal knowledge	Institutional knowledge
Open the kimono	Full disclosure, Provide insight into

Source: PYPL
Published: July 2020

Popular programming languages

The PYPL Popularity of Programming Languages Index is created by analyzing how often language tutorials are searched on Google:

the more a language tutorial is searched,
the more popular the language is assumed to be.

If you believe in collective wisdom, the index can help you decide which language to study, or which one to use in a new software project.

Rank	Language	Share
1	Python	31.8%
2	Java	17.1
3	Javascript	8.0
4	C#	7.0
5	C/C++	6.0
6	PHP	5.6
7	R	4.0
8	Objective-C	2.6
9	Swift	2.3
10	TypeScript	1.9

Source: PYPL
Published: July 2020

Popular programming languages

The PYPL PopularitY of Programming Language Index is created by analyzing how often language tutorials are searched on Google: the more a language tutorial is searched, the more popular the language is assumed to be. It is a leading indicator. The raw data comes from Google Trends.

If you believe in collective wisdom, the PYPL Popularity of Programming Language index can help you decide which language to study, or which one to use in a new software project.

Rank	Language	Share
1	Python	31.8%
2	Java	17.1%
3	Javascript	8.0%
4	C#	7.0%
5	C/C++	6.0%
6	PHP	5.6%
7	R	4.0%
8	Objective-C	2.6%
9	Swift	2.3%
10	TypeScript	1.9%

Source: Izenda
Published: October 2019

May 22, 2020

Relational vs non-relational databases

Relational databases

- Think of an Excel Spreadsheet
- Fits nicely into rows and columns (i.e. schema)
- Stores data in tables
- Called Structured Query Language (SQL) databases

Table 1

Name	Food Preference	Trained
Rufus	Wet	False
Markley	Dry	True

Table 2

Name	Tag Number	Height (in)
Rufus	934	18
Markley	216	22

Table joining 1 and 2

Name	Food preference	Trained	Tag Number	Height (in)
Rufus	Wet	False	934	18
Markley	Dry	True	216	22

Non-relational databases

- Think of a Word Document
- Does not use a tabular schema of rows and columns
- More flexible because data doesn't have to fit into a pre-defined schema
- Called Not Only SQL databases (NoSQL)

Key	Document

1001	{
	"Name": Rufus
	"Attributes": [
	{"Food Preference": Wet,
	"Trained": False,
	}]
	"Tag Number": 934
	}

Source: Izenda
Published: October 2019

Relational vs Non-Relational Databases

Relational databases

- Think of an Excel Spreadsheet
- Fits nicely into rows and columns (i.e., schema)
- Stores data in tables
- Called Structured Query Language (SQL) databases

Table 1

Name	Food Preference	Trained
Rufus	Wet	False
Markley	Dry	True

Table 2

Name	Tag Number	Trained
Rufus	934	18
Markley	216	22

Table joining 1 & 2:

Name	Food Preference	Trained	Tag Number	Height (inches)
Rufus	Wet	False	934	18
Markley	Dry	True	216	22

Non-relational databases

- Think of a Word Document
- Does not use a tabular schema of rows and columns
- More flexible because data doesn't have to fit into a predefined schema
- Called Not Only SQL databases (NoSQL)
- Four types
  - Document-oriented databases
  - Key-Value stores
  - Wide-Column stores
  - Graph stores
- A good rule of thumb: the bigger the data set, the more likely a non-re-lational database is a better fit.

Key	Document
1001	{ "Name": Rufus , "Attributes": [{ "Food Preference": Wet , "Trained": False , }] "Tag Number": 934 }
1002	{ "Name": Markley , "Attributes": [{ "Food Preference": Dry , "Trained": True , }] "Tag Number": 216 }

Source: Money, Stack Exchange
Published: June 2012

Tailwind or headwind?

Originally nautical terms, tailwind and headwind today are financial jargon (often used at Amazon).

Tailwind
↳ if the wind is at your back, it will help you move forward more quickly
↳ a business situation that makes growth less difficult
↳ Example: Falling fuel prices will reduce Amazon Air costs and increase profitability.

Headwind
↳ if moving into a headwind, that will make progress more difficult

↳ a business situation that makes growth more difficult.

↳ Example: An increase in the price of fish will cause Amazon Meal Kit's salmon entree to be less profitable.

↳ From Amazon's Q3 2019 Earnings Call:
"The Japan consumption tax was raised from 8% to 10% on October 1. We expect our [international growth rate] to be a negative headwind of 300 basis points year-over-year in Q4 2019."

— Brian Olsavsky, SVP and CFO at Amazon

Source: Money, StackExchange
Published: June 2012

Tailwind or Headwind?

Originally a nautical term, tailwind and headwind today are financial jargon. If the wind is at your back, a tailwind, that will help you move forward more quickly. If you are moving into a headwind, that will only make progress more difficult.

Tailwinds: a situation that makes growth less difficult.

Example: Falling fuel prices will reduce Amazon Air costs and increase profitability.

Headwinds: a situation that makes growth more difficult.

Example: An increase in the price of fish will cause Amazon Meal Kit's salmon entree to be less profitable.

"The Japan consumption tax was raised from 8% to 10% on October 1st. We expect our [international growth rate] to be a negative headwind of 300 basis points year-over-year in Q4 2019."

> **—Brian Olsavsky, SVP & CFO at Amazon
> said during the Q3 2019 earnings call**

CHAPTER 8

FRAMEWORKS

Source: Farnam Street   October 26, 2020
Published: January 2018

Mental Models: An Overview

Mental models are frameworks for thinking. They simplify complex things so your brain can reason through them. We use mental models to make better decisions without knowing every detail about a situation.

In other words, mental models are thinking tools—shortcuts for reasoning. They help our brain go 'I've seen this type of problem before!'

Charlie Munger, the vice chairman of Berkshire Hathaway believes that "you can't really know anything if you just remember isolated facts... you've got to have models in your head."

While one can find hundreds of mental models, we'll be learning about "FOUR" of them this week.

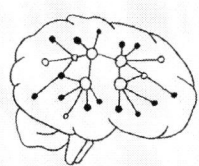

Source: Farnam Street
Published: January 2018

Mental Models: An Overview

Mental models are frameworks for thinking. They simplify complex things so your brain can reason through them. We use mental models to make better decisions without knowing every detail about a situation.

In other words, mental models are thinking tools—shortcuts for reasoning. They help our brain go *'I've seen this type of problem before!'*

Charlie Munger, the vice chairman of Berkshire Hathaway, believes that *"you can't really know anything if you just remember isolated facts... you've got to have models in your head."*

Source: Farnam Street   October 27, 2020
Published: April 2018

Mental Models: First Principles

We use first principles thinking to clarify complicated problems by separating the underlying facts from any assumptions based on them. What remains are the essentials, which we use to ask ourselves: what is the most efficient way to solve a problem if you started from scratch?

Example: Both a chef and a cook can make a meal; however, only the chef relies on first principles.

A chef uses instinct and experience to take raw ingredients and create a meal. She understands the flavor profiles and combinations at such a fundamental level that she doesn't even use a recipe. On the other hand, a cook relies on a pre-defined recipe; he is out of luck without the recipe.

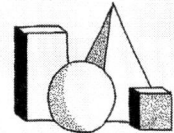

Source: Farnam Street
Published: April 2018

Mental Models: First Principles

We use first principles thinking to clarify complicated problems by separating the underlying facts from any assumptions based on them. What remains are the essentials, which we use to ask ourselves:

What is the most efficient way to solve a problem if you started from scratch?

Example: Both a chef and a cook can make a meal; however, only the chef relies on first principles.

A chef uses instinct and experience to take raw ingredients and create a meal. She understands the flavor profiles and combinations at such a fundamental level that she doesn't even use a recipe. On the other hand, a cook relies on a pre-defined recipe; he is out of luck without the recipe.

Source: Farnam Street   October 28, 2020
Published: April 2016 + March 2017

Mental Models: Second-Order Thinking

When we solve one problem, we can end up unintentionally creating another problem. Second-order thinking is reasoning further ahead to examine the long-term and often unintended consequences of our decisions.

Second-order thinkers improve their decision making by asking themselves: "And then what?"

EXAMPLE: moving to electric cars.

A first-order consequence is that we will replace the fuel tank with a battery.

A second-order consequence is that we will reduce the number of moving parts in a car, thus greatly reducing the frequency of auto repairs needed.
How will this impact car mechanics?

Another second-order consequence is that fuel is bought at gas stations, of which there are about 150k in the US.
What will happen to gas stations?

BONUS: A third-order consequence is that since gas is sold at low-profit margins, these retailers make more money as convenience stores.
What happens to the products such as snacks, soda, and tobacco sold there?

Source: Farnam Street and Benedict Evans
Published: April 2016 and March 2017

Mental Models: Second-Order Thinking

When we solve one problem, we can end up unintentionally creating another problem. Second-order thinking is reasoning further ahead to examine the long-term and often unintended consequences of our decisions.

Second-order thinkers improve their decision making by asking themselves: *"And then what?"*

Example: moving to electric cars

A first-order consequence is that we will replace the fuel tank with a battery.

A second-order consequence is that we will reduce the number of moving parts in a car, thus greatly reducing the frequency of auto repairs needed. *How will this impact car mechanics?*

Another second-order consequence is that fuel is bought at gas stations, of which there are about 150k in the USA. *What will happen to gas stations?*

Bonus: A third-order consequence is that since gas is sold at low-profit margins, these retailers make more money as convenience stores. *What happens to the products such as snacks, soda, and tobacco sold there?*

Source: Cornell
Published: February 2002

Mental Models: Reciprocity

People tend to return a favor. When you offer something first for free, people feel a sense of indebtedness towards you. That's why when a friend invites you to their party; there's an obligation for you to invite them to a future party you are hosting.

EXAMPLE: the use of candy to increase restaurant tipping

Researchers found that most people will feel they owe a debt when given a mint for free and will repay it by leaving a higher tip.

When a waiter leaves one after-dinner mint when they drop off your check, you will tip 3% more than if no mint was given. But when the waiter leaves two mints, your tipping increases to 14% more than no mint! To receive a 23% greater tip than no mint, a waiter can drop off one mint, leave, and then come back to your table with a second mint.

Source: Cornell
Published: February 2002

Mental Models: Reciprocity

People tend to return a favor. When you offer something first for free, people feel a sense of indebtedness towards you. That's why when a friend invites you to their party; there's an obligation for you to invite them to a future party you are hosting.

Example: the use of candy to increase restaurant tipping

Researchers found that most people will feel they owe a debt when given a mint for free and will repay it by leaving a higher tip.

When a waiter leaves one after-dinner mint when they drop off your check, you will tip 3% more than if no mint was given. But when the waiter leaves two mints, your tipping increases to 14% more than no mint! To receive a 23% greater tip than no mint, a waiter can drop off one mint, leave, and then come back to your table with a second mint.

Source: Effectiviology   October 30, 2020
Published: August 2018

Hanlon's Razor

"Never attribute to malice that which can be adequately explained by neglect," said Robert Hanlon

Hanlon's Razor teaches us that when we assess other people's actions we should not assume that they acted out of a desire to cause harm. We should look to give others the benefit of the doubt. Doing so helps us avoid the negative emotions associated with assuming bad intentions.

EXAMPLE: you didn't receive a calendar invite to an important event in your organization. Remembering Hanlon's Razor, you recognize that you shouldn't assume that this happened because the person in charge decided to avoid sending it to you since they dislike you. Instead, it is reasonable to assume that they simply forgot to send the invitation.

Source: Effectiviology
Published: August 2018

Mental Models: Hanlon's Razor

"Never attribute to malice that which can be adequately explained by neglect," said Robert Hanlon

Hanlon's Razor teaches us that when we assess other people's actions, we should not assume that they acted out of a desire to cause harm. We should look to give others the benefit of the doubt. Doing so helps us avoid the negative emotions associated with assuming bad intentions.

Example: you didn't receive a calendar invite to an important event in your organization. Remembering Hanlon's Razor, you recognize that you shouldn't assume that this happened because the person in charge decided to avoid sending it to you since they dislike you. Instead, it is reasonable to assume that they simply forgot to send the invitation.

Source: Team Gantt
Published: August 2018

How to clear project confusion with a RACI

A RACI chart is a matrix used to assign roles and responsibilities for milestones of a project. By mapping out ownership, you can eliminate confusion of "Who's doing what?"

Responsible: the owner of completion

Accountable: the one who validates the deliverable before it's deemed complete

Consulted: provider of input; usually have domain expertise

Informed: those who are kept in the loop of project progress

Deliverable	Product Manager	Marketing Manager	Software Developer	User Experience
Display 1-day free delivery option on eligible orders	A	I	R	C
Publish marketing emails and issue Press Release	A	R	I	C
Design Checkout banner to inform Prime Customers	A	C	I	R
Write PR/FAQ	R	I	C	C

Source: Team Gantt
Published: August 2018

How to Clear Project Confusion with a RACI

A RACI chart is a matrix used to assign roles and responsibilities for milestones of a project. By mapping out ownership, you can eliminate confusion of *"who's doing what?"*.

Responsible: The team member owning completion.

Accountable: The one who validates the deliverable before it's deemed complete.

Consulted: The people who provide input; usually have domain expertise.

Informed: Those who are kept in the loop of project progress.

Example: Free Prime member 1-day shipping launch.

Deliverable	Product Manager	Marketing Manager	Software Developer	User Experience
Display 1-day free delivery option on eligible orders	A	I	R	C
Publish marketing emails and issue Press Release	A	R	I	C
Design checkout banner to inform Prime Customers	A	C	I	R
Write PR/FAQ	R	I	C	C

Source: Future Blind
Published: August 2019

The flywheel effect

Technical definition:
    Positive feedback loops that build momentum,
    increasing the payoff of incremental effort.

Layman's definition:
    When good things you do lead to
    more good things "just happening."

Examples:

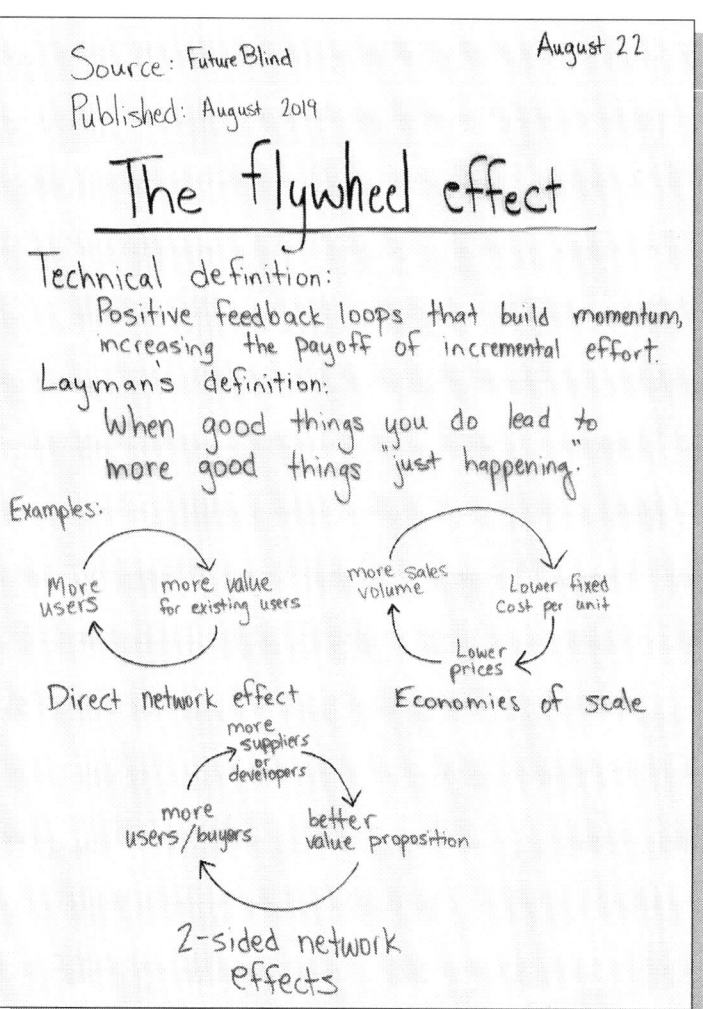

More users → more value for existing users

Direct network effect

more sales volume → Lower fixed Cost per unit → Lower prices

Economies of scale

more suppliers or developers → better value proposition → more users/buyers

2-sided network effects

Source: FutureBlind
Published: August 2019

The Flywheel Effect

Technical definition: Positive feedback loops that build momentum, increasing the payoff of incremental effort.

Layperson's definition: When good things you do lead to more good things "just happening".

Examples:

- **Direct network effect:** more users -> more value for existing users
- **Economies of scale:** more sales volume -> lower fixed cost per unit -> lower prices
- **2-sided network effect:** better value prop -> more users -> more developers

Source: The Observer Effect   October 12, 2020
Published: October 2020

On Good Meetings

"A great meeting has three key elements:

1. the desired outcome of the meeting is clear ahead of time
2. the various options are clear, ideally ahead of time
3. the roles of the participants are clear all the time

I often find that meetings lack one of those elements.

The largest source of optimization for a company is the makeup of their meetings. It's not about fewer meetings because meetings serve a purpose. Rather, it's key to improve the meetings, themselves.

A lot of my efforts focus on teaching people this framework."

- Daniel Ek, CEO of Spotify

Source: The Observer Effect
Published: October 2020

On Good Meetings

From Daniel Ek, the CEO of Spotify:

"A great meeting has three key elements:

1. the desired outcome of the meeting is clear ahead of time
2. the various options are clear, ideally ahead of time
3. the roles of the participants are clear at the time

I often find that meetings lack one of those elements.

The largest source of optimization for a company is the makeup of their meetings. It's not about fewer meetings because meetings serve a purpose. Rather, it's key to improve the meetings themselves.

A lot of my efforts focus on teaching people this framework."

Source: Live Plan
Published: November 2016

SWOT Analysis

Use SWOT Analysis to assess your organization's current position before you decide on any new strategy. SWOT stands for strengths, weaknesses, opportunities, and threats.

Strengths and weaknesses are things that you have some control over and can change (internal).

Opportunities and threats are things that you cannot change but can react to that go on outside your company (external).

EXAMPLE:
Markley's Dog Daycare

Strengths	Weaknesses
#1 Location: convenient for dog drop off	#1 Scheduling: clients are double-booked often
#2 Brand: Customers love the origin story	#2 Lack of experience: only 3 months in business
Opportunities	**Threats**
#1 Growing: the pet industry is growing year-over-year	#1 On-demand: Competitors are offering dog walks booked via mobile app.
#2 Grooming: a new service customers ask for	#2 Holiday surge: too much demand can lead to disappointed customers

Source: LivePlan
Published: November 2016

SWOT Analysis

Use SWOT Analysis to assess your organization's current position before you decide on any new strategy. SWOT stands for Strengths, Weaknesses, Opportunities, and Threats.

Strengths and weaknesses are things that you have some control over and can change (internal).

Opportunities and threats are things that you cannot change but can react to that go on outside your company (external).

Example: Markley's Dog Daycare

Strengths
Location: convenient for dog drop off
Brand: customers love the origin story

Weaknesses
Scheduling: clients double-booked often
Lack of experience: only 3 months in business

Opportunities
Growing: the pet industry is growing year-over-year
Grooming: a new service customers ask for

Threats
On-demand: competitors are offering dog walks booked via an app
Holiday surge: too much demand can lead to disappointed customers

Source: McKinsey
Published: December 2009

The Three Horizons framework

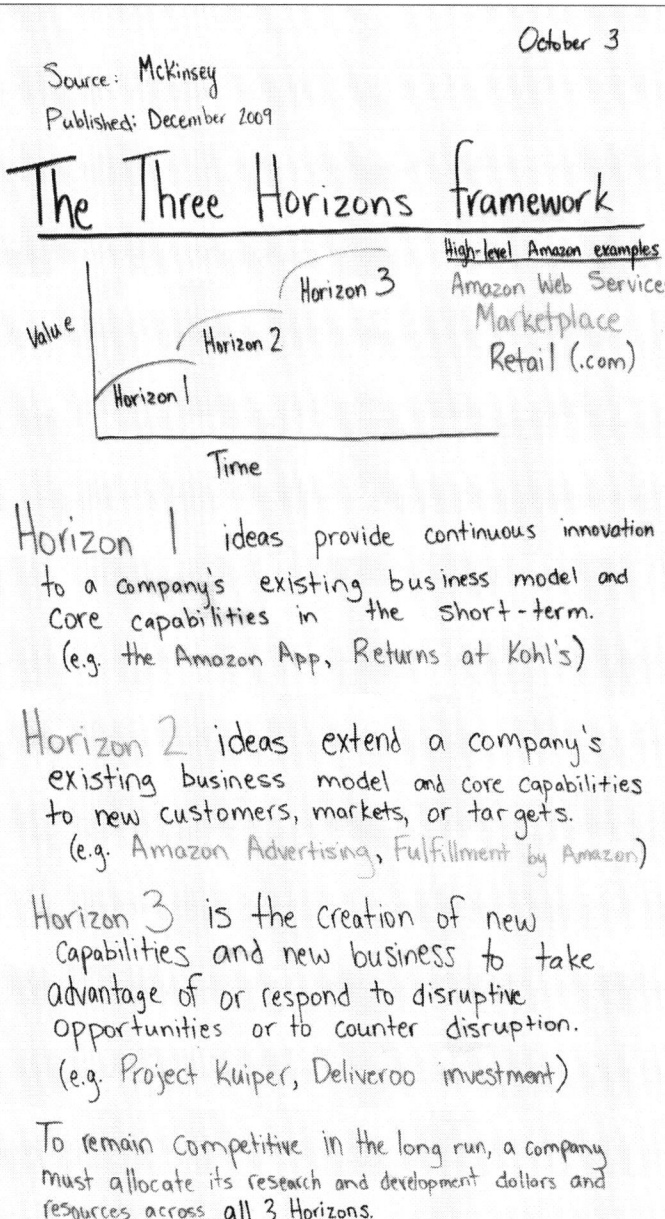

High-level Amazon examples
Amazon Web Services
Marketplace
Retail (.com)

Horizon 1 ideas provide continuous innovation to a company's existing business model and core capabilities in the short-term.
(e.g. the Amazon App, Returns at Kohl's)

Horizon 2 ideas extend a company's existing business model and core capabilities to new customers, markets, or targets.
(e.g. Amazon Advertising, Fulfillment by Amazon)

Horizon 3 is the creation of new capabilities and new business to take advantage of or respond to disruptive opportunities or to counter disruption.
(e.g. Project Kuiper, Deliveroo investment)

To remain competitive in the long run, a company must allocate its research and development dollars and resources across all 3 Horizons.

Source: McKinsey
Published: December 2009

The Three Horizons Framework

High-level Amazon examples:

- **Horizon 1:** Retail (.com)
- **Horizon 2:** Marketplace
- **Horizon 3:** Amazon Web Services (AWS)

Horizon 1 ideas provide continuous innovation to a company's existing business model and core capabilities in the short-term. (e.g., the Amazon App, Returns at Kohl's)

Horizon 2 ideas extend a company's existing business model and core capabilities to new customers, markets, or targets. (e.g., Amazon Advertising, Fulfillment by Amazon)

Horizon 3 is the creation of new capabilities and new business to take advantage of or respond to disruptive opportunities or to counter disruption. (e.g., Project Kuiper, Deliveroo investment)

McKinsey suggests that to remain competitive in the long run, a company must allocate its research and development dollars and resources across all three horizons.

Source: Getting Things Done
Published: January 2011

June 24, 2020

Horizons of Focus

The Horizons of Focus is a framework for aligning your daily actions with long-term visions and goals.

Horizon 5: Purpose and principles
- Answer the question, "Why are we doing this?"
- Think a team off-site meeting

Horizon 4: Vision
- Define what it will look, sound, and feel like with successful implementation
- Focus on long-term outcomes and ideal scenarios
- Think a 6-page PR/FAQ

Horizon 3: Goals
- What needs to be accomplished within 12 months to make the vision happen
- Think annual planning and quarterly recalibration

Horizon 2: Areas of accountability
- Spheres of work required to move forward
- Think organization charts and defined responsibilities (e.g, RACI)

Horizon 1: Projects
- Deliverables that we want to achieve in less than 12 months
- Think project plan and weekly business reviews

Ground: Actions on your calendar
- A single task that is part of a project.
- Think of an item on your to-do list

Source: Getting Things Done
Published: January 2011

Horizons of Focus

The Horizons of Focus is a framework for aligning your daily actions with your long-term visions and goals.

Horizon 5: *Purpose and Principles*

- Answer the question, "why are we doing this?"
- Think a team off-site meeting

Horizon 4: *Vision*

- Define what it will look, sound, feel like with successful implementation
- Focus on long-term outcomes and ideal scenarios
- Think a 6-page PR/FAQ

Horizon 3: *Goals*

- What needs to be accomplished within 12 months to make the vision happen
- Think annual planning with quarterly recalibration

Horizon 2: *Areas of accountability*

- Spheres of work required to move forward
- Think organization charts and defined responsibilities (e.g., RACI)

Horizon 1: *Projects*

- Deliverables that we want to achieve in less than 12 months
- Think project plan and weekly business reviews

Ground: *Actions on your calendar*

- A single task that is part of a project
- Think of an item on your to-do list

Source: Harvard Business Review
Published: March 2015

July 15, 2020

Red and Blue Oceans

The book "Blue Ocean Strategy" argues that lasting success comes not from battling competitors but from creating blue oceans – untapped new market spaces ripe for growth. The red ocean represents bloody fighting by rival competitors over a shrinking profit pool.

Red Ocean Strategy	Blue Ocean Strategy
Compete in an existing, known market space / industry.	Create a new, uncontested market space.
Cut-throat competition that turns the ocean red with blood.	Unexplored by competition vast, deep, and full of opportunity.
Exploit existing demand, dividing customers between rival companies.	Create new demand by developing uncontested market space.
As competition increases, prospects for profit and growth decline. A zero-sum game.	Opportunity for growth due to innovation.
Examples: AmazonBasics Batteries Ryanair or Southwest Airlines	Examples: Amazon Alexa Cirque du Soleil

Source: Harvard Business Review
Published: March 2015

Red and Blue Oceans

The book "Blue Ocean Strategy" argues that lasting success comes not from battling competitors but from creating blue oceans — untapped new market spaces ripe for growth. The red ocean represents bloody fighting by rival competitors over a shrinking profit pool.

Red Ocean Strategy	Blue Ocean Strategy
Compete in an existing, known market space / industry.	Create a new, uncontested market space.
Cut-throat competition that turns the ocean red with blood.	Unexplored by competition vast, deep, and full of opportunity.
Exploit existing demand, dividing customers between rival companies.	Create new demand by developing uncontested market space.
As competition increases, prospects for profit and growth decline. A zero-sum game.	Opportunity for growth due to innovation.
Example: AmazonBasics Batteries, Ryanair or Southwest Airlines.	**Example: Amazon Alexa, Cirque du Soleil (circus acts).**

Source: 5 Whys
Published: May 2019

Bus factor

The bus factor is the minimum number of team members that have to suddenly disappear from a project before the project stalls and is at risk of falling apart. We prefer the optimistic phrase of won the lottery instead of hit by a bus!

A factor of 1 means that there exists a single source of failure.

A factor of 5 (on a 5 person team) means the risk of the project is low because team members know enough to carry on in the case some of them would quit the project.

You can increase the bus factor by:

- Sharing knowledge
  ↳ e.g., daily huddle meetings, documentation, project update emails

- Cross-training to develop skill redundancy
  ↳ e.g., AWS certifications, team lunch and learn sessions

- Peer-reviewing
  ↳ e.g., code reviews, editing a teammate's PR/FAQ

Source: 5 Whys
Published: May 2019

Bus Factor

The *"bus factor"* is the minimum number of team members that have to suddenly disappear from a project before the project stalls and is at risk of falling apart. We prefer the optimistic phrase of *"won the lottery"* instead of *"hit by a bus."*

A factor of 1 means that there exists a single source of failure. A factor of 5 (on a 5 person team) means the risk of the project is low because team members know enough to carry on in the case some of them would quit the project.

You can increase the bus factor by:

- Sharing knowledge (e.g., daily huddle meetings, documentation, project email updates)
- Cross-training to develop skill redundancy (e.g., AWS certifications, team lunch and learn sessions)
- Peer-reviewing (e.g., code reviews, editing a teammate's PR/FAQ)

Source: Simon Wardley
Published: March 2015

Pioneers, Settlers, Town Planners

This framework describes a way of understanding the unique combination of characteristics and aptitude needed to bring products and services to life.

Pioneers $\xrightarrow{\text{ideas}}$ Settlers $\xrightarrow{\text{ideas}}$ Town Planners

reliable services

Pioneers
- bold thinkers who come up with the new, exciting ideas
- fail often; you wouldn't trust what they build
- innovative ideas uncovered are passed onto the Settlers
- example:
  Jack Kilby who invented the integrated circuit (aka microchip)

Settlers
- they build trust and understanding by listening to customers
- generate revenue while finding product-market fit
- turn ideas from Pioneers into a product
- example:
  Henry Edwards Roberts who invented the first personal computer (Altair 8800)

Town Planners
- take the Settlers' product and scale it to reach more customers
- you can trust the quality of their product
- utilize economies of scale to make things faster and more efficient
- they operate the services that Pioneers build upon
- example: Apple Computer inventing the Macintosh

Source: Simon Wardley
Published: March 2015

Pioneers, Settlers, Town Planners

This framework describes a way of understanding the unique combination of characteristics and aptitude needed to bring products and services to life.

Pioneers

- bold thinkers who come up with new, exciting ideas
- fail often; you wouldn't trust what they build
- innovative ideas uncovered are passed onto the Settlers

    example: Jack Kilby who invented the integrated circuit (aka microchip)

Settlers

- they build trust and understanding by listening to customers
- generate revenue while finding product-market fit
- turn ideas from Pioneers into a product

    example: Henry Edwards Roberts who invented the first PC (Altair 8800)

Town Planners

- take the Settlers' product and scale it to reach more customers
- you can trust the quality of their product
- utilize economies of scale to make things faster and more efficient
- they operate the services that pioneers build upon

    example: Apple Computer inventing the Macintosh

Source: Thought Co
Published: February 2019

Maslow's Hierarchy of Needs

Abraham Maslow was a physiologist who studied positive human qualities and the lives of exemplary people. In 1954 he created the Hierarchy of Human Needs. In this theory, higher needs in the hierarchy begin to emerge when people feel they have sufficiently satisfied the previous one.

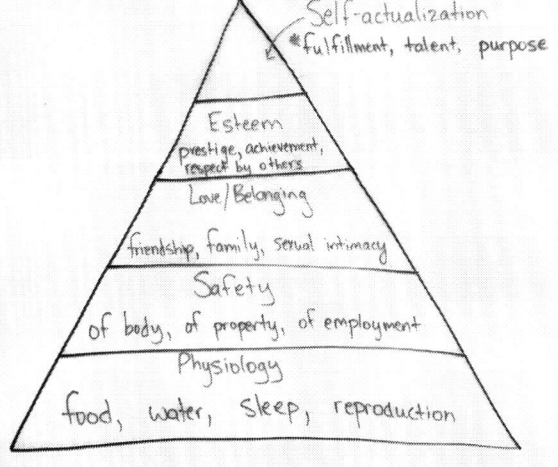

Self-actualization
*fulfillment, talent, purpose

Esteem
prestige, achievement,
respect by others

Love/Belonging
friendship, family, sexual intimacy

Safety
of body, of property, of employment

Physiology
food, water, sleep, reproduction

Source: Thought Co
Published: February 2019

Maslow's Hierarchy of Needs

Abraham Maslow was a physiologist who studied positive human qualities and the lives of exemplary people. In 1954, he created the Hierarchy of Human Needs. In this theory, higher needs in the hierarchy begin to emerge when people feel they have sufficiently satisfied the previous need.

Self-actualization: fulfillment*, talent, purpose

Esteem: prestige, respect by others, achievement

Love/belonging: friendship, family, sexual intimacy

Safety: security of the body, of property, of employment

Physiology: food, water, sleep, reproduction

*Not the ecommerce kind of fulfillment.

Source: Gartner
Published: August 2018

Gartner Hype Cycle

The Gartner Hype Cycle provides a graphic representation of the maturity and adoption of technologies.

Innovation Trigger:

Early proof of concept stories and media interest trigger significant publicity.

Peak of Inflated Expectations:

Early publicity produces a number of success stories — often accompanied by scores of failures.

Trough of Disillusionment:

Interest wanes as experiments and implementations fail to deliver. Producers of the technology shake out or fail.

Slope of Enlightenment:

Benefits are more widely understood. Second- and third-generation products appear from techology providers.

Plateau of Productivity:

Mainstream adoption starts to take off.

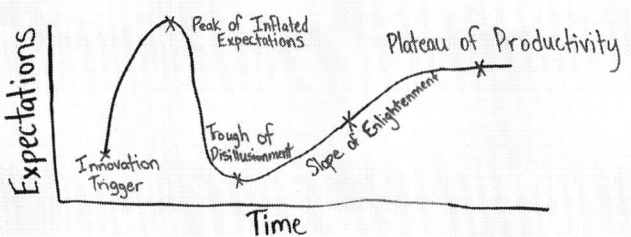

Source: Gartner
Published: August 2018

Gartner Hype Cycle

The Gartner Hype Cycle provides a graphic representation of the maturity and adoption of technologies.

Innovation Trigger: Early proof-of-concept stories and media interest trigger significant publicity.

Peak of Inflated Expectations: Early publicity produces a number of success stories — often accompanied by scores of failures.

Trough of Disillusionment: Interest wanes as experiments and implementations fail to deliver. Producers of the technology shake out or fail.

Slope of Enlightenment: Benefits are more widely understood. Second- and third-generation products appear from technology providers.

Plateau of Productivity: Mainstream adoption starts to take off.

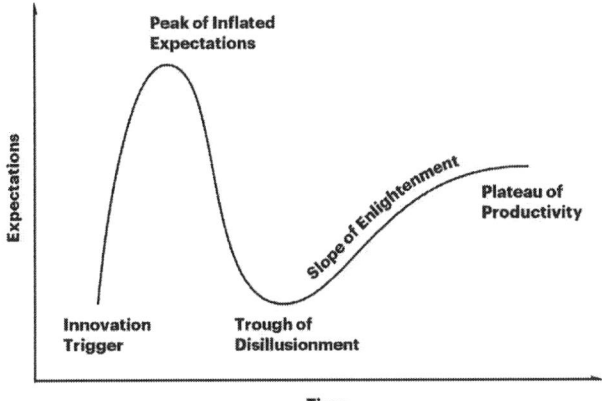

A visual of the Gatner Hype Cycle. Image: Gartner

Source: Gantt.com
Published: February 2010

Using a Gantt chart to manage projects

A Gantt chart is a type of bar chart that illustrates a project schedule. It is a useful way of showing activities displayed against time for planning projects of all sizes. This allows you to see at a glance:

(1) What the activities are (tasks or events)
(2) When each activity begins and ends (duration)
(3) Where activities overlap (dependencies)
(4) The start and end date of the whole project

Task name	Jan	Feb	March	April
Planning				
Research				
Design				
Implementation				
Follow-up				

Source: Gantt.com
Published: February 2010

Using a Gantt Chart to Manage Projects

A Gantt chart is a type of bar chart that illustrates a project schedule. It is a useful way of showing activities displayed against time for planning projects of all sizes. This allows you to see at a glance:

1. What the activities are (tasks or events).
2. When each activity begins and ends (duration).
3. Where activities overlap (dependencies).
4. The start and end date of the whole project.

Task name	Jan	Feb	March	April
Planning	███			
Research		██		
Design			██	
Implementation			██	
Follow-Up				███

Source: Toyota
Published: May 2016

Lean manufacturing

Definition: a Japanese method that relentlessly works to eliminate waste from the manufacturing process without sacrificing productivity.

Pillars of Lean Manufacturing °° (if you like the 7 below, you can find many more!)

Andon: highlighting a problem as it occurs; halts production so that a solution can be found; often activated by a pull-cord or button

Just-In-Time: arranging regular, small deliveries of exactly the correct amount required; saves warehouse space and unnecessary cost-carrying

Kaizen: combining collective talents to standardize procedures and eliminate waste; often performed as a kaizen blitz

Kanban: work items are represented visually on a board, allowing team members to see the state of every piece of work at any time

Muda: any activity or process that does not add value; examples such as transport and waiting time

Hansei: a reflection meeting to recognize mistakes and take appropriate action to avoid re-occurrence

Gemba: taking the time to watch how a process is done and talking with those who do the job; often referred to as a Gemba Walk

Source: Toyota
Published: May 2016

Lean Manufacturing

Definition: a Japanese method that relentlessly works to eliminate waste from the manufacturing process without sacrificing productivity.

Pillars of lean manufacturing
If you like the seven below, there are many more!

Andon: highlighting a problem as it occurs; halts production so that a solution can be found; often activated by a pull-cord or button.

Just-In-Time: arranging regular, small deliveries of exactly the correct amount required; saves warehouse space and unnecessary cost-carrying.

Kaizen: combining collective talents to standardize procedures and eliminate waste; often performed in a kaizen blitz.

Kanban: work items are represented visually on a board, allowing team members to see the state of every piece of work at any time.

Muda: any activity or process that does not add value; examples such as transport and waiting time.

Hansei: a reflection meeting to recognize mistakes and take appropriate action to avoid re-occurrence.

Gemba: taking the time to watch how a process is done and talking with those who do the job; often referred to as a Gemba Walk.

CHAPTER 9

BEHAVIORAL ECONOMICS

Source: Thought Co   December 7, 2020
Published: December 2019

Behavioral Economics: Status quo bias

- What is it?

People often prefer to stay with the status quo because it is familiar and comfortable, whereas change can be costly, risky, or inconvenient. Status quo bias is also known as default bias.

- What are examples?

- Subscribe + Save — Amazon auto-delivers your items on a regular schedule, without having to place a new order each time.

- free trials — after a free trial ends, a subscription service may automatically sign us up for a paid subscription.

- retirement savings — we are more likely to accept the default amount for contributions to a retirement account like a 401(k) than change the value.

- How can we make better decisions?

As a builder, the defaults we set should reflect what most customers would choose given unlimited time and energy to decide for themselves.

As a customer, it's worthwhile to slow down and consider every option when making high-stakes decisions like how much to invest in retirement, which health plan to choose, or whether to become an organ donor.

Source: Thought Co
Published: December 2019

Behavioral Economics:
Status quo bias

What is it?

People often prefer to stay with the status quo because it is familiar and comfortable, whereas change can be costly, risky, or inconvenient. Status quo bias is also known as **default bias.**

What are examples?

- **Subscribe & Save** – Amazon auto-delivers your items on a regular schedule, without having to place a new order each time.
- **free trials** – after a free trial ends, a subscription service may automatically sign us up for a paid subscription.
- **retirement savings** – we are more likely to accept the default amount for contributions to a retirement account like a 401(k) than change the value.

How can we make better decisions?

As a builder, the defaults we set should reflect what most customers would choose given unlimited time and energy to decide for themselves.

As a customer, it's worthwhile to slow down and consider every option when making high-stakes decisions like how much to invest in retirement, which health plan to choose, or whether to become an organ donor.

Source: The Decision Lab   December 8, 2020
Published: May 2020

<u>Behavioral Economics: Mental accounting</u>

- What is it?

Mental accounting is the idea that we assign mental labels to money that cause us to act irrationally while spending it.

- What are examples?

  - at-home coffee – we're willing to pay more for Keurig coffee pods if we think of the pods as a substitute for coffee from a café rather than for inexpensive home-brewed coffee.
  - tax refunds – people saved less of their tax refund check if they were told it was "bonus income," and saved more of the check if it was described as "withheld income."

- How can we make better decisions?

Richard Thaler, who coined the term in 1999, recommends that people treat all money the same regardless of its origin or how they plan to use it.

Source: The Decision Lab
Published: May 2020

Behavioral Economics: Mental accounting

What is it?

Mental accounting is the idea that we assign mental labels to money that cause us to act irrationally while spending it.

What are examples?

- **at-home coffee** – we're willing to pay more for Keurig coffee pods if we think of the pods as a substitute for coffee from a café rather than for inexpensive home-brewed coffee.
- **tax refunds** – people saved less of their tax refund check if they were told it was "bonus income," and saved more of the check if it was described as "withheld income."

How can we make better decisions?

Richard Thaler, who coined the term in 1999, recommends that people treat all money the same, regardless of its origin or how they plan to use it.

Source: Harvard Business Review   December 9, 2020
Published: October 2001

Behavioral Economics: Authority bias

• What is it?

Authority bias describes people's tendency to defer to experts; we tend to give more weight to the opinions of authority figures like doctors, professors, or politicians.

• What are examples?

- Physical therapists increased patient compliance by 34% using simple measures like displaying their awards, diplomas, and certifications in their offices.
- A sales representative can list certifications they've earned in their email signature to persuade customers they're an expert in their field.

• How can we make better decisions?

If you want to be persuasive, clearly display your expertise and certifications; don't be shy, and don't assume it's self-evident.

When you're being persuaded by a notable figure, make sure the source of their authority is relevant; a medical doctor should tell you about health, not the stock market.

Source: Harvard Business Review
Published: October 2001

Behavioral Economics: Authority bias

What is it?

Authority bias describes people's tendency to defer to experts; we tend to give more weight to the opinions of authority figures like doctors, professors, or politicians.

What are examples?

Physical therapists increased patient compliance by 34% using simple measures like displaying their awards, diplomas, and certifications in their offices.

A sales representative can list certifications they've earned in their email signature to persuade customers they're an expert in their field.

How can we make better decisions?

If you want to be persuasive, clearly display your expertise and certifications; don't be shy, and don't assume it's self-evident.

When you're being persuaded by a notable figure, make sure the source of their authority is relevant; a medical doctor should tell you about health (their specialty), not the stock market.

Source: The Decision Lab   December 10, 2020
Published: January 2020

Behavioral Economics: Framing effect

• What is it?

The framing effect is the psychological idea that we process the same piece of information differently depending on how it is framed.

• What are examples?

Version A	Version B
2 out of every 100 patients die as a result of the surgery	the surgery has a 98% survival rate
the service costs $730 a year	you'll only pay $2 a day for the service
20% fat ground beef	80% lean ground beef

• How can we make better decisions?

Framing is a tool of persuasion. Try to reframe a convincing claim in a new way to see if it becomes less compelling if phrased differently. If you want to avoid framing, then explain the rationale behind your decisions, even if you're only explaining them to yourself.

Source: The Decision Lab
Published: January 2020

Behavioral Economics: Framing effect

What is it?

The **framing effect** is the psychological idea that we process the same piece of information differently depending on how it is framed.

What are examples?

Version A	Version B
2 out of every 100 patients die as a result of the surgery	the surgery has a 98% survival rate
the service costs $730 a year	you'll only pay $2 a day for the service
20% fat ground beef	80% lean ground beef

How can we make better decisions?

Framing is a tool of **persuasion**. Try to reframe a convincing claim in a new way to see if it becomes less compelling if phrased differently. If you want to avoid framing, then explain the rationale behind your decisions, even if you're only explaining them to yourself.

Source: Harvard Business Review   December 11, 2020
Published: February 2015

Behavioral Economics: Algorithm aversion

- What is it?

We are often reluctant to trust algorithms to make our decisions for us, and we're quick to lose confidence in algorithms if they make even minor errors—even though they outperform humans on average.

- What are examples?

Although self-driving cars are safer and less likely to make errors than human drivers, many people feel uncomfortable with the idea of self-driving cars on the road.

In one experiment at UPenn, participants examined MBA admissions data to determine the students' academic success during the program. Participants could either submit their own estimates or submit algorithm-generated predictions. Even with the knowledge that the algorithm was superior to human logic, participants tended to make predictions themselves.

- How can we make better decisions?

People trust algorithms more when the user has some level of input (e.g. the ability to tweak the output by 10%), even if the user input actually decreases the algorithm's performance abilities.

Source: Harvard Business Review
Published: February 2015

Behavioral Economics: Algorithm aversion

What is it?

We are often reluctant to trust algorithms to make our decisions for us, and we're quick to lose confidence in algorithms if they make even minor errors–even though they outperform humans on average.

What are examples?

Although self-driving cars are safer and less likely to make errors than human drivers, many people feel uncomfortable with the idea of self-driving cars on the road.

In one experiment at UPenn, participants examined MBA admissions data to determine the students' academic success during the program. Participants could either submit their own estimates or submit algorithm-generated predictions. Even with the knowledge that the algorithm was superior to human logic, participants tended to make predictions themselves.

How can we make better decisions?

People trust algorithms more when the user has some level of input (e.g., the ability to tweak the output by 10%), even if the user input actually decreases the algorithm's performance abilities.

Source: Journal of Marketing Research
Published: October 2011

September 30

A sale on Campbell's soup

To measure the behavior change attributed to a slight change in an advertisement, three supermarkets in Sioux City, Iowa participated in a study. Over multiple days, a sign announcing "Campbell's Soup Sale - 79¢/can" was mounted behind each display of soup. The researchers measured the impact of adding a second line, putting either:

(A) Offer limited to 12 cans per person

OR

(B) No limit per person

Results

The limit of 12 signage increased sales per buyer by 112% compared to the no limit, from 3.3 to 7.0 cans/buyer.

This phenomena is attributed to 2 factors:

(1) Artificial scarcity

(2) Anchoring bias

Source: Journal of Marketing Research
Published: October 2011

A Sale on Campbell's Soup

To measure the behavior change attributed to a slight change in an advertisement, three supermarkets in Sioux City, Iowa participated in a study. Over multiple days, a sign announcing *"Campbell's Soup Sale — 79¢/can"* was mounted behind each display. The signs rotated between *'Offer limited to 12 cans per person'* and *'No limit per person'*.

The limit of 12 signage increased sales per buyer by *112%* compared to the no limit per — from *3.3 cans per buyer* to *7.0 cans per buyer*.

This phenomena is attributed to 2 factors:

1. **Artificial scarcity:** The limited availability of items even though capacity exists to supply them.
2. **Anchoring bias:** When individuals use an initial piece of information to make subsequent judgments.

Social proof

Social proof is the psychological concept that when we feel uncertain, we tend to look to others for answers as to how we should behave and think.

It is driven by the assumption that the surrounding people possess more knowledge about the current situation.

It is problematic in that groups of people can reach suboptimal or even outright wrong decisions driven by a desire to fit in with others (i.e., groupthink).

Examples

1) Theaters and operas in the 1800s would hire a claque, an organized group that would applaud at pre-arranged times, so that the rest of the audience followed.

2) Celebrities will pay for fake social media followers and likes so that they are perceived as more reputable, leading to growth of real followers.

Source: Farnam Street
Published: September 2009

Social Proof

Social proof is the psychological concept that when we feel uncertain, we tend to look to others for answers as to how we should behave and think. It is driven by the assumption that the surrounding people possess more knowledge about the current situation. It is problematic in that groups of people can reach suboptimal or even outright wrong decisions driven by a natural desire to fit in with others (i.e., *groupthink*).

Examples

- Theaters and operas in the 1800s would hire a claque, an organized group that would applaud at pre-arranged times, so that the rest of the audience followed. (Wikipedia)
- Celebrities will pay for fake social media followers and likes so that they are perceived as more reputable, leading to growth of real followers. (NYT)

Source: Journal of Personality and Social Psychology
Published: December 2000
n= 754 shoppers

When choice is demotivating

On one day, shoppers at an upscale food market
saw a display table with 24 varieties of gourmet jam.
Those who sampled the jams received a coupon
for $1 off any jam.

On another day, shoppers saw a similar table except
that only 6 varieties of jam were on display.

The display with 24 varieties attracted
39% more interest than the display with 6.
But when the time came to purchase,
4% of the people who saw the large display
converted compared to 31% of the
people who saw the small display (6 varieties).

Take-aways

- There is diminishing marginal utility in
  having alternatives.
- More choice requires increased time and effort.
- More choice is not always better.

Source: Journal of Personality and Social Psychology
Published: December 2000
n = 754 shoppers

When Choice is Demotivating

On one day, shoppers at an upscale food market saw a display table with 24 varieties of gourmet jam. Those who sampled the spreads received a coupon for $1 off any jam. On another day, shoppers saw a similar table, except that only six varieties of the jam were on display. The large display attracted 39% more interest than the small one. But when the time came to purchase, 4% of the people who saw the large display converted compared to 31% of the people who saw the small display.

There is diminishing marginal utility in having alternatives; each new option subtracts a little from the feeling of well-being. More choice requires increased time and effort and can lead to anxiety, regret, and self-blame if the choices don't work out. When the number of available options is small, these costs are negligible.

"More choice is not always better."

—**Barry Shwartz, author of *The Paradox of Choice***

Source: The Decision Lab   August 25, 2020
Published: July 2020

Escalation of Commitment

Escalation of commitment, also known as commitment bias, occurs when a decision maker continues to devote resources to a failing project instead of cutting losses. Psychologists refer to this behavioral pattern as the "sunk cost fallacy" which is when individuals continue a behavior due to previously invested resources (time, money, or effort).

Example 1: Sony continues to produce electronics despite losing $8.5 billion in over 10 years.

Example 2: The US Air Force failed to develop a combat support software after spending 8 years and $1.1 billion on the project.

Example 3: Stock investors may hold onto a stock longer than would be advantageous, simply because they already committed to the investment.

Source: The Decision Lab
Published: July 2020

Escalation of commitment

Escalation of commitment, also known as commitment bias, occurs when a decision-maker continues to devote resources to a failing project instead of cutting losses. Psychologists refer to this behavioral pattern as the *"sunk cost fallacy,"* which is when individuals continue a behavior due to previously invested resources (time, money, or effort).

Example 1: Sony continues to produce electronics despite losing $8.5 billion in over 10 years.

Example 2: The US Air Force failed to develop a combat support software after spending 8 years and $1.1 billion on the project.

Example 3: Stock investors may hold onto a stock longer than would be advantageous, simply because they already committed to the investment.

Source: Journal of Legal Studies
Published: September 1999

October 18

The Israeli child care experiment

Incentives don't always change behaviors in the way we'd expect.

Background

In a study of day care centers in Israel, economists tried to help schools identify ways to reduce late pick-ups. When parents are tardy, the result is at least one teacher must wait around for the parents to arrive.

Experiment

The economists conducted a study by announcing that any parent arriving more than 10 minutes late would pay a $3 fine.

Outcome

After the fine was enacted, the number of late pickups promptly doubled. As soon as the parents had the option to pay a small fine and avoid the guilt of making a teacher wait, parents took it en masse.

Take-away

This study suggests that effective methods of changing behavior should combine economic, moral, and social incentives.

Source: Journal of Legal Studies
Published: September 1999

The Israeli Childcare Experiment

Incentives don't always change behaviors in the way we'd expect.

Background

In a study of day care centers in Israel, economists tried to help schools identify ways to reduce late pick-ups. When parents are tardy, the result is at least one teacher who must wait around for the parents to arrive.

Experiment

The economists conducted a study by announcing that any parent arriving more than ten minutes late would pay a *$3* fine.

Outcome

After the fine was enacted, the number of late pickups promptly went up by *100%*. As soon as parents had the option to pay a small fine and avoid the guilt of making a teacher wait, they took it en masse.

Take-away

This study suggests that effective methods of changing behavior should combine economic, moral, and social incentives.

Source: Working Out Loud   September 23, 2020
Published: April 2017

The Value of Wine

Years ago, you bought a case of good 2000 Bordeaux for $50 a bottle. It now sells at wine auctions for $125 a bottle.

You decide to drink a bottle with dinner. Which of the following best captures your feeling of the bottle's cost to you?

A. $0 – I already paid for it years ago.

B. $50 – the amount I paid for it.

C. $50+ – the money I paid plus the interest that would have been earned on it.

D. $125 – the amount I could sell it for.

E. $-75 – I saved money because now I get to drink a $125 bottle, but I only paid $50.

*Follow up tomorrow, September 24.

Source: Working Out Loud
Published: April 2017

The Value of Wine

Years ago, you bought a case of good 2000 Bordeaux for $50 a bottle. It now sells at wine auctions for $125 a bottle.

You decide to drink a bottle with dinner. Which of the following best captures your feeling of the bottle's cost to you?

1. $0 — I already paid for it years ago.
2. $50 — the amount I paid for it.
3. $50+ — the money I paid plus the interest that would have been earned on it.
4. $125 — the amount I could sell it for.
5. $-75 — I saved money because now I get to drink a $125 bottle, but I only paid $50.

Turn the page to see how Fact of the Day 1 readers answered.

Source: Fact of the Day 1   September 24, 2020
Published: September 2020

The Value of Wine

Yesterday's fact asked you to assign a value to a bottle of wine that increased in value to $125 since you purchased it 20 years ago for $50.

The results of 5,300 votes:

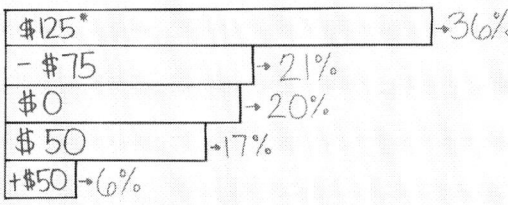

This question was created by behavioral economists Daniel Kahneman, Amos Tversky, and Richard Thaler. The correct answer according to economic theory is $125, since the opportunity cost of drinking the wine is selling it at that price. 64% of us behaved in a different way than what an economist would expect.

Source: *Fact of the Day 1*
Published: September 2020

The Value of Wine (Part 2)

Yesterday's fact asked you to assign a value to a bottle of wine that increased in value to $125 since you purchased it 20 years ago for $50.

The results of 5,300 votes:

- *36% responded $125*
- *21% responded -$75*
- *20% responded $0*
- *17% responded $50*
- *6% responded $50+*

This question was created by behavioral economists Daniel Kahneman, Amos Tversky, and Richard Thaler. The correct answer according to economic theory is $125, since the opportunity cost of drinking the wine is selling it at that price. 64% of us behaved in a different way than what an economist would expect.

CHAPTER 10

COMMUNICATION

Amazon Writing Style Tip

use time efficiently: make sentences clear and concise

- Use subject-verb-object sentences with "doers" and "action"
- Avoid long sentences (30+ words)
- Avoid "clutter" words + phrases

Bad Example		Better
with the possible exception of	→	except
due to the fact that	→	because
totally lacked the ability to	→	could not
until such time as	→	until
for the purpose of	→	for

Source: Des Traynor
Published: March 2018

Amazon Writing Style Tips

Use time efficiently: make sentences concise & direct.

- Use subject-verb-object sentences with "doers" and "action"
- Avoid long sentences (30+ words)
- Avoid "clutter" words/phrases

Bad Example		Better
With the possible exception of	→	except
Due to the fact that	→	because
Totally lacked the ability to	→	could not
Until such time as	→	until
For the purpose of	→	for

Source: David Perell
Published: December 2019

July 21, 2020

Tips for business writers

- Replace adjectives **with** numbers.

AWS has launched a lot of services in a decade. → The number of AWS services has grown from 18 in 2011 to 200+ in 2020.

- Make sentences concise.

Due to the fact that → because

- Write out acronyms the first time you use them.

→ The framework for the AWS Well-Architected Tool (WA Tool) was updated to respond to user feedback.

- Vary your sentence length.

→ Keep sentences less than 30 words.

- Avoid weasel words that create an impression of meaning.

Should result in benefits in the next couple of weeks. → I expect a 4% reduction in customer service tickets for cold deliveries over the next 14 days.

Examples:
. significantly worse, often, some people, evidence suggests

Source: David Perell
Published: December 2019

Tips for Business Writers

Replace adjectives with numbers.

AWS has launched a lot of services in a decade.	→	The number of AWS services has grown from 18 in 2011 to 200+ in 2020.

Make sentences concise.

Due to the fact that	→	because

Write out acronyms the first time you use them.

- The Framework for the AWS Well-Architected Tool (WA Tool) was updated to respond to user feedback.

Vary your sentence length.

- Keep sentences less than 30 words.

Avoid weasel words that create the impression of meaning.

(Examples: significantly worse, often, some people, evidence suggestions)

"Should result in benefits in the next couple of weeks."	→	"I expect 4% reduction in customer service tickets for cold deliveries over the next 14 days.

Communicating Status at Amazon

RED

You have a high degree of confidence that your project cannot meet its objectives and goal dates.

The team has worked to identify mitigations to solve key blockers but those have
  failed
      or
do not exist.

YELLOW

Your project has one or more launch blocking items and there is no mitigation in place. You are working to identify potential mitigations and have not yet concluded that none exist.

If you fail to identify mitigations, then RED.

If you identify them, then GREEN.

GREEN

Your project has a well defined plan of execution, has resources assigned to it, and your resources are executing per the plan. Your project may have risks; however, you have identified appropriate mitigations for those risks.

Source: Harvard Business Review
Published: April 2013

Communicating Status at Amazon

RED: You have a high degree of confidence that your project cannot meet its objectives and goal date. The team has worked to identify mitigations to solve key blockers but those have failed or do not exist.

YELLOW: Your project has one or more launch blocking items and there is no mitigation in place. You are working to identify potential mitigations and have not yet concluded that none exist.

If you fail to identify mitigations, then **RED**.

If you identify them, then **GREEN**.

GREEN: Your project has a well-defined plan of execution, has resources assigned to it, and your resources are executing per the plan. Your project may have risks; however, you have identified appropriate mitigations for those risks.

Source: Workfront

Published: October 2019

September 21, 2020

State of Work

3,750 respondents in the US, UK, Netherlands, and Germany were surveyed to learn about knowledge workers' perspectives on work management and employee success.

- Wasteful meetings (62%) and excessive emails (53%) are the top activities preventing work from getting done

- Workers are interrupted by collaboration tools (e.g., Slack and Amazon Chime) an average of 14 times each work day

- 93% said it should be as easy to find information at work as it is to find information on Google

- 91% crave modern technology solutions (e.g., automating repetitive tasks)

Source: Workfront
Published: October 2019

State of Work

3,750 respondents in the US, UK, Netherlands, and Germany were surveyed to learn about knowledge workers' perspectives on work management and employee success.

- Wasteful meetings (62%) and excessive emails (53%) are the top activities preventing work from getting done
- Workers are interrupted by collaboration tools (e.g., Slack and Amazon Chime) an average of 14 times each work day
- 93% said it should be as easy to find information at work as it is to find information on Google
- 91% crave modern technology solutions (e.g., automating repetitive tasks)

Source: Harvard Business Review   January 15, 2020
Published: January 2019

Breaking the email obsession

The average professional spends 28% of the work day reading and answering email.
That amounts to 2.6 hours spent and 120 messages received per day.

Professionals check their email inbox an average of 15 times per day, or every 37 minutes, yet only 8% of coworkers expect a response within an hour.

Practices to break the inbox habit

- Turn off notifications and instead check your email hourly

- Move every email out of your inbox the first time you read it.

- Use the search functionality with operators to re-find emails

- Avoid processing irrelevant or less important emails individually by setting up rules

Source: Harvard Business Review
Published: January 2019

Breaking the Email Obsession

The average professional spends *28%* of the work day reading and answering email — that amounts to *2.6 hours* spent and *120 messages* received per day. Professionals check their email inbox an average of *15 times* per day, or every *37 minutes*, yet only *8%* of coworkers expect a response within an hour.

Practices to break the inbox habit:

- Turn off notifications and instead check your email hourly.
- Move every email out of your inbox the first time you read it.
- Use the search functionality with search operators to re-find emails.
- Avoid processing irrelevant or less important emails individually by setting up rules.

Source: Fact of the Day 1   October 6, 2020
Published: September 2020

Know your Audience

Work backwards from your audience before you begin writing.

Take a moment to consider:

- Whom are you writing for?
- What is important to your audience when it comes to your topic?
- What words do they use when they talk about the subject?

Purpose for Writing	Audience	Tone
funding proposal (e.g., OPI)	investors general managers	persuasive format, thoughtful
promotion assessment	people managers	sincere, empathetic
process documentation (e.g., SOP)	operations associates	direct, pragmatic, procedural
a daily fact delivered via email	life-long learners, business enthusiasts	fun informal

Source: Fact of the Day 1
Published: September 2020

Know Your Audience

Work backwards from your audience before you begin writing.

Take a moment to consider:

- Whom are you writing for?
- What is important to your audience when it comes to your topic?
- What words do they use when they talk about the subject?

Purpose for Writing	Audience	Tone
funding proposal (e.g., OP1)	investors general managers	persuasive, formal, thoughtful
promotion assessment	people managers	sincere, empathetic
process documentation (e.g., SOP)	operations associates	direct, pragmatic, procedural
a daily fact delivered via email	life-long learners, business enthusiasts	fun, informal

Source: Clear Voice   September 18, 2020

Published: April 2019

Narrative arc

Whether you're writing an operating plan (e.g., OP1), a children's book, or a pitch for a startup, employing a narrative arc helps your reader follow your story.

Exposition – the background information, such as historical context.

Rising Action – a conflict that gives rise to the main purpose of your writing.

Climax – the most exciting or important part of the story, the main point.

Freytag's Pyramid

Falling action – the de-escalation of tension or conflict to make way for the conclusion.

Resolution – the ending point where the story ties up neatly.

Example:

Amazon Echo's commercial "Cooking Together" is a 30 second ad that uses the narrative arc.

Exposition: a woman burns a duck she's cooking and uses the Alexa video calling feature to ask her father for help.

Rising Action: her father instructs her as she puts together a new meal.

Climax: the woman quickly puts together a beautiful pasta dinner.

Falling Action: dinner is ready, the doorbell rings, and her dad asks "what's his name?"

Resolution: "Alexa, hang up" and as she walks to get the door, we see "Dinner with Sam" on her Echo Show's home screen.

Source: Clear Voice
Published: April 2019

Narrative arc

Whether you're writing an operating plan (e.g., OP1), a children's book, or a pitch for a startup, employing a narrative arc helps your reader follow your story.

Exposition — the background information, such as historical context.

Rising action — a conflict that gives rise to the main purpose of your writing.

Climax — the most exciting or important part of the story, the main point.

Falling action — the de-escalation of tension or conflict to make way for the conclusion.

Resolution — the ending point where the story ties up neatly.

Example: Amazon Echo's commercial **"Cooking Together"** is a 30-second ad that uses the narrative arc.

Exposition: a woman burns a duck she's cooking and uses the Alexa video calling feature to ask her father for help.

Rising Action: her father instructs her as she puts together a new meal.

Climax: the woman quickly puts together a beautiful pasta dinner.

Falling Action: dinner is ready, the doorbell rings, and her dad asks, "what's his name?"

Resolution: "Alexa, hang up," and as she walks to get the door, we see "Dinner with Sam" on her Echo Show's home screen.

Source: Reedsy   October 8, 2020
Published: October 2019

Types of Irony

Irony is a storytelling tool used to contrast how things seem and how they are in reality. Irony brings added layers and texture to a story and comes in three categories:

Type of Irony	Explanation	Example
Situational	When you expect one outcome to occur, but the opposite occurs.	• A fire department burns down • A critic of social media uses. Facebook to share their criticisms • An unsinkable ship "The Titanic" sinks on its first voyage.
Dramatic	When the audience knows more about what is going on than the characters.	• In Star Wars, Luke does not know Darth Vader is his father until Episode V, but the audience knows sooner. • In Romeo and Juliet, Romeo does not know that Juliet has faked her death, so he decides to drink poison to take his own life.
Verbal	When you say something but mean the opposite.	• In The Catcher in the Rye, Holden Caulfield casually says, "I have to have this operation. It isn't very serious. I have this tiny little tumor on the brain." • In Shakespeare's Julius Caesar, Brutus is described as "an honorable man" when Brutus conspired to assassinate Caesar.

Source: Reedsy
Published: October 2019

Types of Irony

Irony is a storytelling tool used to contrast how things seem and how they are in reality. Irony brings added layers and texture to a story and comes in three categories:

Type of Irony	Explanation	Example
Situational	When you expect one outcome to occur, but the opposite occurs.	• A fire department burns down, A critic of social media uses Facebook to share their criticisms. • An unsinkable ship "The Titanic" sinks on its first voyage.
Dramatic	When the audience knows more about what is going on than the characters.	• In Romeo and Juliet, Romeo does not know that Juliet has faked her death, so he decides to drink poison and take his own life.
Verbal	When you say something, but mean the opposite.	• In The Catcher in the Rye, Holden Caulfield casually says, "I have to have this operation. It isn't very serious. I have this tiny little tumor on the brain." • In Shakespeare's Julius Caesar, Brutus is described as "an honorable man" when Brutus conspired to assassinate Caesar.

CHAPTER 11

EMOTIONAL INTELLIGENCE (EQ)

Source: Harvard Adult Development Study   August 8
Published: April 2017

Lessons from the longest study on happiness

In 1938 during the Great Depression Harvard researchers started tracking the lives of 268 Harvard sophomores. The idea was to track the development through periodic interviews and medical checkups, with the aim of revealing clues to leading happy and healthy lives.

(including eventual President, John F. Kennedy!)

The main take-aways from Robert Waldinger: (study Director)

- Loneliness kills. It's as powerful as smoking or alcoholism.
- The people who were most satisfied in their relationships at age 50 were the healthiest at age 80.
- Taking care of your body is important, but tending to your relationships is a form of self-care too.

6 factors that predicted healthy aging:

- Physical activity
- Absence of alcohol abuse
- Absence of smoking
- Having mature mechanisms to cope with life's ups and downs
- Healthy body weight
- Stable marriage

Source: Harvard Adult Development Study
Published: April 2017

Lessons from the Longest Study on Happiness

In 1938 during the Great Depression, Harvard researchers started tracking the lives of *268 Harvard sophomores*. The idea was to track the development through periodic interviews and medical checkups, with the aim of revealing clues to leading healthy and happy lives.

The main take-aways from Robert Waldinger (Study Director):

- "Loneliness kills. It's as powerful as smoking or alcoholism."
- "The people who were the most satisfied in their relationships at age 50 were the healthiest at age 80."
- "Taking care of your body is important, but tending to your relationships is a form of self-care too. That, I think, is the revelation."

6 factors that predicted healthy aging:

- Physical activity
- Absence of alcohol abuse
- Absence of smoking
- Having mature mechanisms to cope with life's ups and downs
- A healthy body weight
- A stable marriage

Among the original recruits were eventual President John F. Kennedy.

Source: Dr. Gary Chapman   September 3, 2020
Published: June 1995

 The Five Love Languages

In his 1992 book, Dr. Gary Chapman outlines five ways that romantic partners express and experience love. According to Chapman's theory, each person has one primary and one secondary love language.

❤ Words of affirmation: Compliments, appreciation, and encouragement mean the world to you, and hearing the words "I love you" are essential.

❤ Quality time: Giving your undivided attention. You prioritize active listening, eye contact, and focused conversations.

❤ Receiving gifts: Gifts convey thoughtfulness and effort. It's not about the monetary value but the symbolic thinking behind the item.

❤ Acts of service: Going out of your way to make your partner's life easier. You ease their burden of responsibilities, such as bringing soup when sick or fixing the Wi-Fi when the internet is down.

❤ Physical touch: Physical presence is crucial. Nonverbal acts such as hugs and holding hands express concern, care, and excitement.

Source: Dr. Gary Chapman
Published: June 1995

The Five Love Languages

In his 1992 book, Dr. Gary Chapman outlines five ways that romantic partners express and experience love. According to Chapman's theory, each person has one primary and one secondary love language.

Words of affirmation: Compliments, appreciation, and encouragement mean the world to you, and hearing the words "I love you" are essential.

Quality time: Giving your undivided attention. You prioritize active listening, eye contact, and focused conversations.

Receiving gifts: Gifts convey thoughtfulness and effort. It's not about the monetary value but the symbolic thinking behind the item.

Acts of service: Going out of your way to make your partner's life easier. You ease their burden of responsibilities, such as bringing soup when sick or fixing the wifi when the internet is down.

Physical touch: Physical presence is crucial. Nonverbal acts such as hugs and holding hands express concern, care, and excitement.

Source: Google
Published: September 2016

April 15, 2020

Understanding team effectiveness

Researchers at Google sought out to answer
What makes a team effective at Google?
They found that what really mattered was less about
who is on the team, and more about how
the team worked together. In order of importance:

Psychological safety: team members feel safe to
take risks and be vulnerable in front of each other.

Dependability: team members get things done
on time and insist on high quality standards.

Structure: team members have clear
roles, plans, and goals.

Meaning: work is personally important to
team members

Impact: team members think their work
matters and creates change.

Variables not significantly connected to team effectiveness:
- Colocation of teammates (sitting together in the same office)
- Concensus-driven decision making   · Team size
- Seniority   · Tenure

Source: Google
Published: September 2016

Understanding Team Effectiveness

Researchers at Google sought out to answer "What makes a team effective at Google?" They found that what really mattered was less about who is on the team, and more about how the team worked together. In order of importance:

Psychological safety: team members feel safe to take risks and be vulnerable in front of each other.

Dependability: team members get things done on time and insist on high quality standards.

Structure: team members have clear roles, plans, and goals.

Meaning: work is personally important to team members.

Impact: team members think their work matters and creates change.

Variables *not* significantly connected to team effectiveness:

- Colocation of teammates (sitting together in the same office)
- Consensus-driven decision making
- Seniority
- Team size
- Tenure

Source: Deloitte
Published: February 2020

August 14, 2020

Business Chemistry's four types

Business Chemistry is Deloitte's system for understanding similarities and differences in work styles so co-workers can create stronger working relationships and tap into team strengths. While most people are a mix of the four, we tend to lean heavily towards one type over the others.

Pioneers value possibilities and spark creativity. They tend to be outgoing, spontaneous, adaptable, and imaginative.

Drivers value challenges and generate momentum. They tend to be quantitative, logical, competitive, and experimental.

Guardians value stability and bring order and rigor. They tend to be reserved, practical, detail-oriented, and methodical.

Integrators value connections and draw teams together. They tend to be diplomatic, empathetic, relationship-oriented, and non-confrontational.

Source: Deloitte
Published: February 2020

Business Chemistry's four types

Business Chemistry is Deloitte's system for understanding similarities and differences in work styles so co-workers can create stronger working relationships and tap into team strengths. While most people are a mix of the four, we tend to lean heavily towards one type over the others.

Pioneers value possibilities and spark creativity. They tend to be outgoing, spontaneous, adaptable, and imaginative.

Drivers value challenges and generate momentum. They tend to be quantitative, logical, competitive, and experimental.

Guardians value stability and bring order and rigor. They tend to be reserved, practical, detail-oriented, and methodical.

Integrators value connection and draw teams together. They tend to be diplomatic, empathetic, relationship-oriented, and non-confrontational.

Source: TED
Published: January 2019

October 15, 2020

Offering Heartfelt Praise

It only takes a bit more effort to turn a vague comment into the kind of praise that could make someone's day, says Cheryl Ferguson, a high school music educator in Winnipeg, Canada.

Here are the three basic components of every effective compliment:

1. Use their name - indicate that the other person is worth your time and worth knowing.

2. Be specific - make your compliment as specific as possible. There's a world of difference between "good job on the memo" and "your third paragraph tied your initiative to the goals of the team and made it easier for me to see the bigger picture."

3. Try not to praise and run - follow up your compliment with a question, such as "what part of the memo did you learn the most writing?" or "what surprised you about the findings?"

Source: TED
Published: January 2019

Offering Heartfelt Praise

It only takes a bit more effort to turn a vague comment into the kind of praise that could make someone's day, says Cheryl Ferguson, a high school music educator in Winnipeg, Canada. Here are the three basic components of every effective compliment.

1. **Use their name** — indicate that the other person is worth your time and worth knowing.
2. **Be specific** — make your compliment as specific as possible. There's a world of difference between "good job on the memo" and "your third paragraph tied your initiative to the goals of the team and made it easier for me to see the bigger picture."
3. **Try not to praise and run** — follow up your compliment with a question, such as "what part of the memo did you learn the most writing?" or "what surprised you about the findings?"

Source: Conscious Leadership   September 30, 2020
Published: September 2020

Lead with Love

"At Whole Foods Market, before we end any meeting, we ask a question: Would anyone like to appreciate a fellow team member?

Whether it's a store team meeting or a strategy session with the executive leadership team, we never leave without opening the floor for people to honor one another's positive contributions.

It's one of the ways we strive as a company to operationalize a virtue that's too often overlooked in business: love."

-John Mackey, CEO of Whole Foods Market

Source: Conscious Leadership
Published: September 2020

Lead with Love

"At Whole Foods Market, before we end any meeting, we ask a question: Would anyone like to appreciate a fellow team member?

Whether it's a store team meeting or a strategy session with the executive leadership team, we never leave without opening the floor for people to honor one another's positive contributions.

It's one of the ways we strive as a company to operationalize a virtue that's too often overlooked in business: **love.***"*

—John Mackey, CEO of Whole Foods Market

Source: Ernst and Young

Published: May 2019
n=1,000 employed U.S. adults

January 17, 2020

The importance of belonging

Researchers found that 39% of respondents say that when colleagues check in with them about how they are doing, both personally and professionally, they feel the greatest sense of belonging at work.

Take away: By reaching out on a personal level we can make colleagues feel significantly more valued and connected.

Where employees feel the greatest sense of belonging:

Workplace	34%
Neighborhood communities	19
Places of worship	17
Other	30

Take away: Businesses have never had a bigger responsibility and opportunity to build community.

Source: Ernst & Young
Published: May 2019
n = 1,000 employed US adults

The Importance of Belonging

Researchers found that *39%* of respondents say that when colleagues check in with them about how they are doing, both personally and professionally, they feel the greatest sense of belonging at work.

Take away: By reaching out on a personal level, we can make colleagues feel significantly more valued and connected.

Where employees feel the greatest sense of belonging:

- **Workplace —** *34%*
- **Neighborhood communities —** *19%*
- **Places of worship —** *17%*

Take away: Businesses have never had a bigger responsibility and opportunity to build community.

SECTION 3

LEARN AND BE CURIOUS

CHAPTER 12

DATA AND PRIVACY

Source: Dataiku   June 1, 2020
Published: April 2020

Key data science Concepts

Machine learning: programming systems to perform a task without coding rule-based instructions

Deep learning: a subset of machine learning where systems can learn hidden patterns from data

Model: a representation of the real world using mathematics

Algorithm: a set of rules used to make a calculation

Training set: a dataset used to find potentially predictive relationships used to create a model

Test set: a dataset with the same structure as the training set used to measure the performance of models

Training: the process of creating a model from the training set

Target: a dependent variable that is the output that a model predicts e.g., the price of a house

Feature: an independent variable that is a measurable piece of data e.g., # of bathrooms in a house

Overfitting: a model that corresponds too closely with a particular set of data (i.e., training set) and may fail to fit additional data (i.e., test set)

Source: Dataiku
Published: April 2020

Key Data Science Concepts

- **Machine Learning**: programming systems to perform a task without coding rule-based instructions
- **Deep Learning**: a subset of ML where systems can learn hidden patterns from data
- **Model**: a representation of the real world using mathematics
- **Algorithm**: a set of rules used to make a calculation
- **Training set**: a dataset used to find potentially predictive relationships used to create a model
- **Test set**: a dataset with the same structure as the training set used to measure the performance of models
- **Training**: the process of creating a model from the training set
- **Target**: a dependent variable that is the output that a model predicts (e.g., price of a house)
- **Feature**: an independent variable that is a measurable piece of data (e.g., # of bathrooms in a house)
- **Overfitting**: a model that corresponds too closely with a particular set of data (i.e., training set) and may fail to fit additional data (i.e., test set)

Source: Computed   September 11, 2020
Published: June 2020

Analytics Maturity

Hindsight

1.- Descriptive analytics: the foundation of analytics; it asks "what happened?"

ex. "How many X did I sell today?"

2.-Diagnostic analytics: draws insight from past data to inform the present.

ex. "Did I sell more or less X on a certain day of the week?"

Insight

3.- Predictive: analyzes predictive models, and potential outcomes to prepare for the future.

ex. "What am I going to sell next week?"

4.-Prescriptive: synthesizes a plan of action or next step using previous analytics.

Foresight

ex. "How can I sell the most X?"

Source: Computd
Published: June 2020

Analytics Maturity

1. **Descriptive analytics:** the foundation of analytics; it asks "what happened?"

   ex., *"How many X did I sell today?"*

2. **Diagnostic analytics:** draws insight from past data to inform the present.

   ex., *"Did I sell more or less X on a certain day of the week?"*

3. **Predictive:** analyzes predictive models, and potential outcomes to prepare for the future.

   ex., *"What am I going to sell next week?"*

4. **Prescriptive:** synthesizes a plan of action or next step using previous analytics.

   ex., *"How can I sell the most X?"*

Source: Kaggle   January 8, 2020
Published: December 2019
n = 4,141 data scientists

The state of data science

Kaggle is an online community, of
data scientists and machine learners. *(Kaggle was acquired by Google in 2017.)*
Respondents are currently employed as data scientists
and could select all responses that apply.

- 84% identify as male.

- 65% are 22-34 years old.

- 72% read blogs, the most popular
  way to learn while working.

- 98% of respondents said they
  continuously learn.

- The most popular interactive development
  environments are:
  83% Jupyter, 38% RStudio, 34% PyCharm

Source: Kaggle
Published: December 2019
n = 4,141 data scientists

The State of Data Science

Kaggle is an online community of data scientists and machine learners. They were acquired in 2017 by Google. Respondents are currently employed as data scientists and could select all responses that apply.

- *84% identify as male.*
- *65% are 22–34 years old.*
- *72% read blogs, the most popular way to learn while working.*
- *98% of respondents said they continuously learn.*
- The most popular interactive development environments are *83% Jupyter, 38% RStudio,* and *34% Py-Charm.*

Source: Pew Research
Published: **November** 2019
n = 4,272 U.S. adults

January 24, 2020

Privacy and control over personal information

Prevalence of tracking

- 62% of respondents feel it is not possible to go through daily life without companies collecting data about them.
- 63% said the same for the government

Not feeling in control of personal data

- Respondents say they have very little or no control over the data that the government (84%) or companies (81%) collect about them.

Rewards of data collection

- 81% think the potential risks of data collection by companies outweigh the benefits.
- 72% say they personally benefit very little or none from company data collection about them.

Security of personal information

"My personal information is ____ than it was 5 years ago."

more secure	about the same	less secure
6%	24%	70%

Source: Pew Research
Published: November 2019
n = 4,272 U.S. adults

Privacy and Control Over Personal Information

Prevalence of tracking: *62%* of respondents feel it is not possible to go through daily life without companies collecting data about them. *63%* said the same for the government.

Not feeling in control of personal data: Respondents say they have very little or no control over the data that the government (*84%*) or companies (*81%*) collect about them.

Rewards of data collection: *81%* think the potential risks of data collection by companies outweigh the benefits. *72%* say they personally benefit very little or none from company data collection about them.

Security of personal information: *70%* feel that their personal information is less secure than five years ago, *24%* feel that it is about the same, and *6%* feel that it is more secure.

Source: Verizon   September 14, 2020
Published: June 2020

Data Breach Investigations Report

The more you know about the cyberthreats you face, the better you can keep your data secure and protect hard to earn customer trust. In a 2020 report, Verizon analyzed 3,950 cofirmed privacy breaches and found the following:

96% of breaches were virtual. Physical actions (like plugging in a flash drive) were present in only 4% of breaches.

86% of breaches are financially motivated. The rest are motivated by espionage for fun, or due to a grudge.

72% of breaches involved large business victims. 28% involved small business victims.

70% of breaches are perpetrated by external actors. The other 30% were performed by internal actors, such as employees.

43% of breaches were attacks on web applications; more than double the number from 2019. As workflows move to cloud services (such as AWS) attackers do too. The most common method of attacking web apps is using stolen or brute-forced credentials.

Source: Verizon
Published: June 2020

Data Breach Investigations Report

The more you know about the cyberthreats you face, the better you can keep your data secure and protect hard to earn customer trust. In a 2020 report, Verizon analyzed 3,950 confirmed privacy breaches and found the following:

- *96% of breaches were virtual. Physical actions (like plugging in a flash drive) were present in only 4% of breaches.*
- *86% of breaches are financially motivated. The rest are motivated by espionage, for fun, or due to a grudge.*
- *72% of breaches involved large business victims. 28% involved small business victims.*
- *70% of breaches are perpetrated by external actors. The other 30% were performed by internal actors, such as employees.*
- *43% of breaches were attacks on web applications; more than double the number from 2019. As workflows move to cloud services (such as AWS) attackers do too. The most common method of attacking web apps is using stolen or brute-forced credentials.*

Source: Webroot   August 31, 2020
Published: November 2018

Social Engineering

Social engineering is the art of manipulating people into giving up confidential information. Criminals often use social engineering tactics as it can be easier to take advantage of humanity's natural inclination to trust than it is to hack software.

One type of social engineering is a phishing attack where a scammer imitates a trusted source to create a seemingly logical scenario for the victim to hand over confidential information.

Tips to avoid being a victim:

- Slow down. Spammers want you to act fast, so they often convey a sense of urgency.
- Double check links. Hover over a link to see the URL before clicking – especially for external senders.
- Beware of attachments, especially if you aren't expecting a file from the sender.

Source: Webroot
Published: November 2018

Social Engineering

Social engineering is the art of manipulating people into giving up confidential information. Criminals often use social engineering tactics as it can be easier to take advantage of humanity's natural inclination to trust than it is to hack software.

One type of social engineering is a **phishing attack**, where a scammer imitates a trusted source to create a seemingly logical scenario for the victim to hand over confidential information.

Tips to avoid being a victim

- **Slow down**. Spammers want you to act fast, so they often convey a sense of urgency.
- **Double-check links**. Hover over a link to see the URL before clicking — especially for external senders.
- **Beware of attachments**, especially if you aren't expecting a file from the sender.

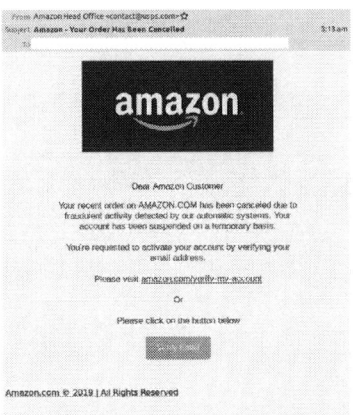

In the example, with the subject 'Amazon – Your Order Has Been Cancelled'
the recipient is advised that "Your recent order on AMAZON.COM has
been cancelled due to fraudulent activity detected." Image: Mailguard.

Source: AndPlus
Published: January 2018

Levels of autonomy

To help automotive engineers, governments, and insurers get a better handle on this new technology, the Society of Automotive Engineers (SAE) defined the five levels of automobile autonomy.

Level 0: Not autonomy; the driver performs all driving tasks.

Level 1: A single function automated; e.g., cruise control

Level 2: Acceleration and steering are automated.
The driver must remain engaged and monitor the vehicle at all times.
e.g., automated lane centering
collision-avoidance braking

Level 3: All safety functions are automated, but the driver may need to take over in an emergency; e.g., Tesla's autopilot feature

Level 4: The vehicle performs all driving functions under certain conditions; e.g., dry, warm weather Human input optional.

Level 5: The vehicle is capable of performing all driving functions under all conditions. No human required.

Source: AndPlus
Published: January 2018

Levels of Autonomy

To help automotive engineers, governments, and insurers get a better handle on this new technology, the Society of Automotive Engineers (SAE) defined the five levels of automobile autonomy.

Level 0: Not autonomy; the driver performs all driving tasks.

Level 1: A single function automated. e.g., cruise control

Level 2: Acceleration and steering are automated. The driver must remain engaged and monitor the vehicle at all times. e.g., automated lane centering and collision-avoidance braking

Level 3: All safety functions are automated, but the driver may need to take over in an emergency; e.g., Tesla's autopilot feature.

Level 4: The vehicle performs all driving functions under certain conditions; e.g., dry, warm weather. Human input optional.

Level 5: The vehicle is capable of performing all driving functions under all conditions. No human required.

Published: March 2019

What is 5G? An executive summary

5G (fifth generation cellular network) is a set of rules for a cellular network instructing how to exchange data using radio frequencies, computer chips, and antennas.

4G vs 5G

	4G	5G
Download speed	0.1 gb/s	1.4 gb/s
Time to download a typical movie	360 seconds	17 seconds
Latency (lag time)	50-200 milliseconds	1-5 milliseconds

Source: DigitalTrends
Published: March 2019

What is 5G? An Executive Summary

5G (fifth-generation cellular network) is a set of rules for a cellular network instructing how to exchange data using radio frequencies, computer chips, and antennas.

Download speed

- **4G** — 0.1 gb/s
- **5G** — 1.4 gb/s

Downloading a typical movie

- **4G** — 360 seconds
- **5G** — 17 seconds

Latency (lag time)

- **4G** — 50 to 200 milliseconds
- **5G** — 1 to 5 milliseconds

CHAPTER 13

ARTIFICIAL INTELLIGENCE

Source: Alteryx

Published: October 2019

Feature engineering

Machine learning uses features which are measurable properties of the object you're trying to analyze. An example is using the number of bedrooms of a house (the feature) to predict the value of the house (the target).

Feature engineering is creating new features from your existing ones to improve predictive model accuracy. Here is an example of using the feature of flight date and time to predict the target of flight status.

Before feature engineering ⟶ After feature engineering

Record	Date and time		Status	Record	Hour of day	Weekend	Status
1	3/20/20	8:20	On time	1	8	No	On time
2	3/20/20	20:00	Delayed	2	20	No	Delayed
3	3/21/20	6:30	On time	3	6	Yes	on time
4	3/21/20	23:10	Delayed	4	23	Yes	Delayed

The insight suggested from this example is that to predict a flight status, hour of day is likely to be a strong indicator of whether a flight is on time or delayed.

Source: Alteryx
Published: October 2019

Feature Engineering

Machine learning uses features which are measurable properties of the object you're trying to analyze. An example is using the number of bedrooms of a house (the feature) to predict the value of the house (the target).

Feature engineering is creating new features from your existing ones to improve predictive model accuracy. Here is an example of using the feature of flight date and time to predict the target of flight status.

Before feature engineering:

Record	Date and Time	Status
1	3/20/20 8:20	On time
2	3/20/20 20:00	Delayed
3	3/21/20 6:30	On time
4	3/21/20 23:10	Delayed

After feature engineering:

Record	Hour of day	Weekend	Status
1	8	No	On time
2	20	No	Delayed
3	6	Yes	On time
4	23	Yes	Delayed

The insight suggested from this example is that to predict a flight status, hour of day is likely to be a strong indicator of whether a flight is on time or delayed.

Source: Machine Learning Mastery   January 3, 2020
Published: March 2016

Supervised and Unsupervised Machine Learning

Supervised learning is like learning with a teacher. From historical data, we know correct answers that have happened. There are two types:

- A classification problem is when the algorithm predicts a category like, an email is spam or not.

- A regression problem is when the algorithm predicts a value like, like how many minutes it will take to drive home from work.

Unsupervised learning is when there are no correct answers and there is no teacher. Algorithms are left to discover interesting structure in the data you provide. There are two types:

- A clustering problem is where you want to group data, like separating news articles into a specified number of topics.

- An association problem is where you want to find rules that are generally true, like customers who buy bagels also tend to buy cream cheese.

Source: Machine Learning Mastery
Published: March 2016

Supervised and Unsupervised Machine Learning

Supervised learning is like learning with a teacher. From historical data, we know correct answers that have happened. There are two types:

- A **classification** problem is when the algorithm predicts a category, like an email is spam or not spam.
- A **regression** problem is when the algorithm predicts a value, like how many minutes it will take to drive home from work.

Unsupervised learning is when there are no correct answers and there is no teacher. Algorithms are left to discover interesting structure in the data you provide. There are two types:

- A **clustering** problem is where you want to group data, like separating news articles into a specified number of topics.
- An **association** problem is where you want to find rules that are generally true, like customers who buy bagels also tend to buy cream cheese.

Source: Monkey Learn
Published: September 2019

August 24, 2020

TOPIC MODELING

Analyzing vast amounts of data - for example, from social media posts, chats, and open-ended survey responses - is not an easy task for a human.

Luckily, we can turn to machine learning (ML) to help. Topic modeling is an unsupervised ML technique capable of scanning a set of documents and determining common themes or topics.

Example:
Using Amazon Comprehend you can scan 100,000 customer reviews of dog treats to identify popular topics mentioned by customers. A manufacturer may find that "smelly", "great for training", and "bite-sized" are the most commonly used phrases, informing them of how to improve the product for future customers.

Source: MonkeyLearn
Published: September 2019

Topic Modeling

Analyzing vast amounts of data — for example, from social media posts, chats, and open-ended survey responses — is not an easy task for a human.

Luckily, we can turn to machine learning (ML) to help. Topic modeling is an unsupervised ML technique capable of scanning a set of documents and determining common themes or topics.

Example

Using Amazon Comprehend, you can scan 100,000 customer reviews of dog treats to identify popular topics mentioned by customers. A manufacturer may find that "smelly," "great for training," and "bite-sized" are the most commonly used phrases, informing them of how to improve the product for future customers.

Source: Path Mind

Published: December 2019

Generative adversarial networks (GANs)

GANs are deep neural net architectures comprised of two nets, pitting one against the other (thus the "adversarial"). GANs can learn to mimic any distribution of data, such as: images, music, speech, and prose.

The generator neural network generates new data.

Think art forger who tries to forge a painting.

The discriminator neural network evaluates the data for authenticity.

Think art investigator who tries to detect imitations.

To see a GAN in action, generate a human face algorithmically:

ThisPersonDoesNotExist.com

Source: Path Mind
Published: December 2019

Generative Adversarial Networks (GANs)

GANs are deep neural net architectures comprised of two nets, pitting one against the other (thus the "adversarial"). GANs can learn to mimic any distribution of data, such as: images, music, speech, and prose.

- The generator neural network generates new data. *(Think art forger who tries to forge a painting.)*
- The discriminator neural network evaluates the data for authenticity. *(Think art investigator who tries to detect imitations.)*

To see a GAN in action, generate a human face algorithmically:
ThisPersonDoesNotExist.com. Image: Philip Wang

Source: MIT Tech Review
Published: April 2020

May 21, 2020

Tiny AI

Artificial intelligence (AI) has historically relied on cloud service provider data centers to process powerful algorithms. A new trend, called Tiny AI, is changing that.

We can now run AI algorithms on our phones. The benefits for existing services (e.g. autocorrect) include faster results without having to ping the cloud to access deep-learning models. Localized AI is also better for privacy since your data no longer needs to leave your device.

These advances are starting to become available to consumers, such as:

Google Assistant that can now run on a user's phone without sending requests to a remote server.

Apple running Siri's speech recognition capabilities and its QuickType keyboard locally on the iPhone.

Source: MIT Tech Review
Published: April 2020

Tiny AI

Artificial intelligence (AI) has historically relied on cloud service provider data centers to process powerful algorithms. A new trend, called Tiny AI, is changing that.

We can now run AI algorithms on our phones. The benefits for existing services (e.g., autocorrect) include faster results without having to ping the cloud to access deep-learning models. Localized AI is also better for privacy since your data no longer needs to leave your device.

These advances are starting to become available to consumers, such as:

Google Assistant that can now run on a user's phone without sending requests to a remote server.

Apple running Siri's speech recognition capabilities and its QuickType keyboard locally on the iPhone.

Source: Gartner

March 24, 2020

Published: July 2019

n= 106 Gartner Research Circle members

Challenges of AI and ML

Artificial intelligence (AI) applies advanced analysis and logic-based techniques including machine learning (ML) to interpret events, support and automate decisions, and to take actions. A survey exploring top challenges to AI and ML adoption within organizations revealed:

Challenge	% of respondents
Skills of staff	56%
Understanding benefits and uses	42
Data scope and quality	34
Finding use cases	26
Integration complexity	26
Defining the strategy	25
Security or privacy concerns	20
Measuring the value	17
Governance issues or concerns	13
Finding funding	12

Source: Gartner
Published: July 2019
n = 106 Gartner Research Circle members

Challenges of AI and ML

Artificial intelligence (AI) applies advanced analysis and logic-based techniques including machine learning (ML) to interpret events, support and automate decisions, and to take actions. A survey exploring top challenges to AI and ML adoption within organizations revealed:

Challenge	% of respondents
Skills of staff	56%
Understanding AI benefits and uses	42%
Data scope and quality	34%
Finding use cases	26%
Integration complexity	26%
Defining the strategy	25%
Security or privacy concerns	20%
Measuring the value	17%
Governance issues or concerns	13%
Finding funding	12%

Source: Allen Institute
Published: July 2019

China's growth in Artificial Intelligence research

Chinese researchers are projected to over-take their U.S. counterparts next year in the share of high-impact papers* published on Artificial Intelligence.

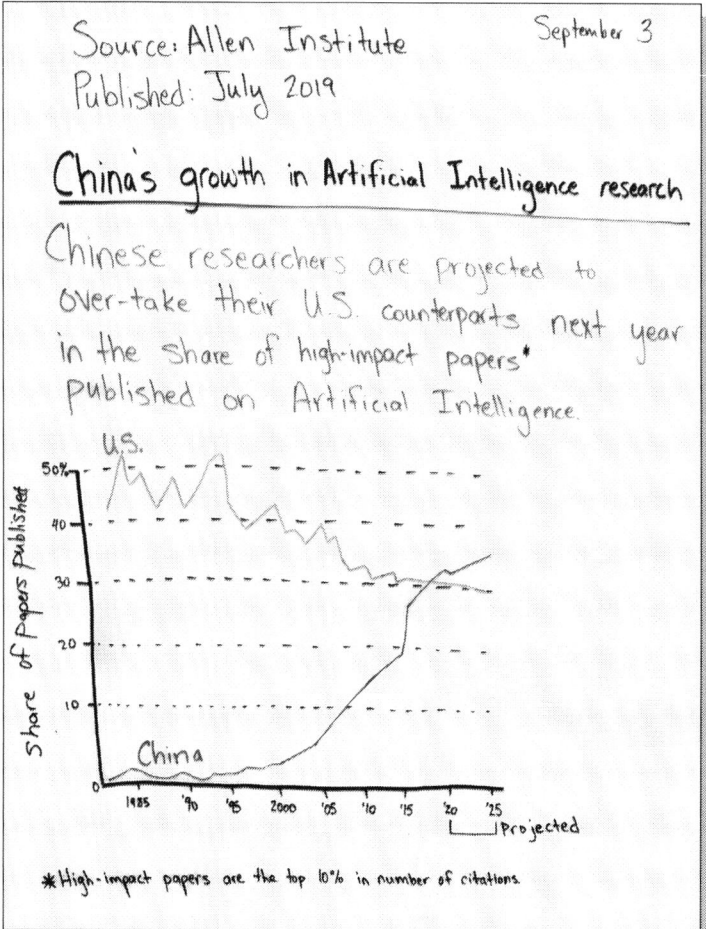

*High-impact papers are the top 10% in number of citations.

Source: Allen Institute for Artificial Intelligence
Published: July 2019

China's Growth in Artificial Intelligence Research

Chinese researchers are projected to over-take their US counterparts next year in the share of high-impact papers* published on Artificial Intelligence.

Year	U.S.	China
1990	48%	1%
2000	39%	2%
2010	35%	13%
2020**	32%	33%
2025**	31%	38%

High-impact papers are defined as the top 10% in terms of number of citations.

**Projected*

CHAPTER 14

ECOMMERCE AND RETAIL

Source: American Consumer Satisfaction Index
(ACSI)

March 21

Published: Feb. 2019

E-com product quality satisfaction

ACSI asked more than 62,000 consumers
to choose their favorite stores in a number
of categories. The satisfaction rate is based
on product quality and is measured on a
scale of 0-100. Overall ecommerce scores
dropped 2.4%. Year-over-year Amazon
dropped 4.0%.

Retailer	Satisfaction Rating
Costco	83
Amazon	82
Target	80
Walmart	74

#1 since 2010. First time as #2. → Amazon

Source: American Customer Satisfaction Index
(ACSI)
Published: February 2019
n = 62,000 US customers

E-com Product Quality Satisfaction

ACSI asked more than *62,000* consumers to choose their favorite stores in a number of categories. The satisfaction rating is based on product quality and is measured on a scale of 0–100. Overall ecommerce scores dropped *2.4% YoY* with Amazon dropping *4%*.

Retailer	Satisfaction Rating
Costco	83
Amazon	82
Target	80
Walmart	74

Source: Baymard Institute
Published: March 2019
n = 2,584 U.S. adults

July 19

Reasons for cart abandoment during checkout

"Have you abandoned any online purchases during the checkout process in the past 3 months? If so, for what reasons?"

↳ can select more than 1 option

Extra costs too high (shipping, tax, fees)	55%
The site wanted me to create an account	34%
Too long/complicated checkout process	26%
I couldn't see/calculate total order cost upfront	21%
I didn't trust the site with my credit card	17%
Website had errors	17%
Delivery was too slow	16%
Return policy wasn't satisfactory	11%
There weren't enough payment methods	6%
The credit card was declined	4%

Source: Baymard Institute
Published: March 2019
n = 2,584 U.S. adults

Reasons for Abandonments During Checkout

Have you abandoned any online purchases during the checkout process in the past 3 months? If so, for what reasons? (Respondents could select multiple responses.)

1. **Extra costs too high (shipping, tax, fees)** — 55%
2. **The site wanted me to create an account** — 34%
3. **Too long / complicated checkout process** — 26%
4. **I couldn't see / calculate total order cost up-front** — 21%
5. **I didn't trust the site with my credit card information** — 17%
6. **Websites had errors / crashed** — 17%
7. **Delivery was too slow** — 16%
8. **Return policy wasn't satisfactory** — 11%
9. **There weren't enough payment methods** — 6%
10. **Credit card was declined** — 4%

Source: Statista

Published: March 2019

n = 2,000 U.S. respondents

Factors driving purchasing decisions on Amazon

In the research, U.S. Amazon buyers indicated which factors are very important in their buying decisions on Amazon.

Factor	Percent
Price	82%
Low shipping cost	70
Positive product reviews	57
Flexible return policy	49
Fast shopping time	47
Prime eligibility	35
Brand name	27

Source: Statista
Published: March 2019
n = 2,000 U.S. respondents

Factors Driving Purchasing Decisions on Amazon

In the research, U.S Amazon buyers indicated which factors are "*very important*" in their buying decisions on Amazon.

Factor	% of respondents
Price	82%
Low shipping cost	70%
Positive product reviews	57%
Flexible return policy	49%
Fast shopping time	47%
Prime eligibility	35%
Brand name	27%

Source: Jungle Scout
Published: February 2020
n= 1,046 Amazon sellers

February 26, 2020

About Amazon sellers

Why sell on Amazon (could select multiple)
- 43% New income stream to replace current
- 41% Flexibility to work anywhere and travel
- 24% Curious to try selling
- 20% To add a sales channel to an existing business
- 18% To earn extra money

Employment status
- 37% employed, full time
- 21% Selling on Amazon only
- 18% employed, part time
- 5% retired
- 3% student
- 16% other

Fulfillment method
- 66% Fulfillment by Amazon (FBA) only
- 6% Fulfillment by Merchant (FBM) only
- 28% FBA and FBM

Business models (could select multiple)
- 71% Private label: sellers create own product label/brand
- 26% Wholesale: sellers buying from a brand or distributor to resell
- 20% Retail arbitrage: sellers buying in physical stores to resell
- 15% Online arbitrage: sellers buying in online stores to resell
- 8% Dropshipping: sellers buying from a supplier who ships directly to the customer
- 6% Handmade: sellers crafting their own products to sell

Source: Jungle Scout
Published: February 2020
n = 1,046 Amazon sellers

About Amazon Sellers

Why sell on Amazon:

Sellers could select multiple

- 43% New income stream to replace current
- 41% Flexibility to work anywhere and travel
- 24% Curious to try selling
- 20% To add a sales channel to an existing business
- 18% To earn extra money

Employment status:

- 37% employed, full time
- 21% Selling on Amazon only
- 18% employed, part time
- 5% retired
- 3% student
- 16% other

Fulfillment method:

- 66% Fulfillment by Amazon (FBA) only
- 6% Fulfillment by Merchant (FBM) only
- 28% FBA and FBM

Business models of Amazon Sellers:

Sellers could select multiple

- 71% Private label: sellers create own product label/brand
- 26% Wholesale: sellers buying from a brand or distributor to resell
- 20% Retail arbitrage: sellers buying in physical stores to resell
- 15% Online arbitrage: sellers buying in online stores to resell
- 8% Dropshipping: sellers buying from a supplier who ships directly to the customer
- 6% Handmade: sellers crafting their own products to sell

Source: YPulse   May 7
Published: June 2018
n = 27k 13-36 year olds

Born
1995-2015   Most Trusted Brands (U.S.)
                              Born 1980 - 1994

Gen Z Rank	Brand	Millenial Rank	Brand
1	Oreo	1	Nike
2	Nike	2	Hershey's
3	Hershey's	3	Amazon
4	Kraft Mac + Cheese	4	Oreo
5	Little Debbie	5	Target
6	M+M's	6	M+M's
7	Amazon	7	Google
8	Under Armour	8	Heinz Ketchup
9	Levi's	9 (tied)	PayPal
10	Apple	9	The North Face

Source: YPulse
Published: June 2018
n = 27K 13–36 year olds

The 10 Brands Millennials and Gen Z Trust the Most (U.S.)

Gen Z (1995 to 2015)

1. Oreo
2. Nike
3. Hershey's
4. Kraft Mac & Cheese
5. Little Debbie
6. M&MS
7. **Amazon**
8. Under Armour
9. Levi's
10. Apple

Millenial (1980 to 1994)

1. Nike
2. Hershey's
3. **Amazon**
4. Oreo
5. Target
6. M&Ms
7. Google
8. Heinz Ketchup
9. PayPal
10. The North Face

Source: Morning Consult   February 19, 2020
Published: January 2020
n= 2,200 U.S. adults

The state of brand trust

Top performing brands including Amazon and Google are more well-trusted than most other institutions, public figures, and ideas.

The share of Americans who say they trust each of the following a lot to do the right thing:

Top 5		Bottom 5	
Your primary doctor	50%	Hollywood	4%
The military	44	Wall Street	5
Amazon	39	The U.S. government	7
Google	38	The news media	8
Extreme weather warnings	36	Capitalism	14

Source: Morning Consult
Published: January 2020
n = 2,200 U.S. adults

The State of Brand Trust

Top-performing brands including *Amazon* and *Google* are more well-trusted than most other institutions, public figures, and ideas. The share of Americans who say they trust each of the following "*a lot*" to do the right thing:

Top Brands	Percent of Americans
Your primary doctor	50%
The military	44%
Amazon	39%
Google	38%
Extreme weather warnings	36%

Bottom 5	
Capitalism	14%
The news media	8%
The U.S. government	7%
Wall Street	5%
Hollywood	4%

Source: 2PM, Web Smith   May 21
Published: May 2019

"Digitally native vertical brands are maniacally focused on the customer experience and they interact, transact, and story-tell to consumers primarily on the web."
    — Bonobos founder and CEO, Andy Dunn

While often started online, they can extend to a brick-and-mortar manifestation. Unlike typical e-commerce companies, digitally native vertical brands control their own distribution.

25 Popular digitally native vertical brands

How many have you bought from?

Warby Parker	The Honest Company
Rent the Runway	Kylie Cosmetics
Anker	Stitch Fix
Peloton	MVMT Watches
Dollar Shave Club	Allbirds
Harry's Inc	Shinola
Birchbox	Hello Fresh
Boxed	Blue Apron
Glossier	Home Chef
Casper	
Tuft and Needle	

Source: 2PM, Web Smith
Published: May 2019

Digitally Native Vertical Brands and their "Maniac Focus" on the Customer Experience

"Digitally native vertical brands are maniacally focused on the customer experience and they interact, transact, and story-tell to consumers primarily on the web."

— Bonobos founder and CEO Andy Dunn.

While often started online, they can extend to a brick-and-mortar manifestation. Unlike typical ecommerce companies, digitally native vertical brands control their own distribution.

25 popular DNVBs:

- Warby Parker
- Rent the Runway
- Anker
- Peloton
- Dollar Shave Club
- Harry's Inc
- Birchbox
- Boxed
- Glossier
- Casper
- Tuft & Needle
- The Honest Company
- Kylie Cosmetics
- StitchFix
- MVMT Watches
- Allbirds
- Shinola
- HelloFresh
- Blue Apron
- Home Chef

Source: CNBC
Published: November 2019

Alibaba's Singles' Day

On November 11th each year, Alibaba hosts their Singles' Day shopping blitz.

Also known as "Double Eleven", the festival's name originates from the calendar date, with the four ones of 11/11 signifying being single.

Sales hit $1 billion in 68 seconds and reached $12 billion in 60 minutes (+22% yoy).

Alibaba expects 500 million users to participate (+100 million users yoy).

For comparison, in Amazon's 2-day Prime Day event sales amounted to $7.2 billion in 2019, according to Statista.

Source: CNBC
Published: November 2019

Alibaba's Singles' Day

On November 11th each year, Alibaba hosts their Singles' Day shopping blitz. Also known as *"Double Eleven"*, the festival's name originates from the calendar date, with the four ones of 11/11 signifying being single.

Sales hit *$1 billion in 68 seconds* and reached *$12 billion in the first 60 minutes (+22% YoY)*. Alibaba expects *500 million users* to participate in the shopping festival (*+100 million users YoY*).

For comparison, in Amazon's 2-day Prime Day event sales amounted to *$7.2 billion in 2019*, according to Statista.

Source: Cowen and Company
Published: October 2018

Retail square footage per person

United States	23.5
Canada	16.8
Australia	11.2
United Kingdom	4.6
Japan	4.4
Netherlands	4.1
France	3.8
Switzerland	3.6
Spain	3.4
China	2.8
Italy	2.8
Taiwan	2.4
Thailand	2.3
Germany	2.3
South Korea	2.2
Russia	1.4
Indonesia	1.0

Source: Cowen and Company
Published: October 2018

Retail Square Footage Per Person

US	23.5
Canada	16.8
Australia	11.2
UK	4.6
Japan	4.4
Netherlands	4.1
France	3.8
Switzerland	3.6
Spain	3.4
China	2.8
Italy	2.8
Taiwan	2.4
Thailand	2.3
Germany	2.3
South Korea	2.2
Russia	1.4
Indonesia	1.0

Source: Field Agent
Published: September 2019
n = 1,497 US holiday shoppers

Top US gift retailers

"When purchasing holiday gifts this year, which 3 retailers will probably receive most of your spending? Choose up to 3." - survey question

Retailer	Likelihood
Amazon.com	64%
Walmart	62
Target	44
Kohl's	17
Best Buy	10
T.J. Maxx	9
Bath and Body Works	9
Costco	8
Macy's	8
Sam's Club	6
GameStop	6

Source: Field Agent
Published: September 2019
n = 1,497 holiday hoppers

Top US Gift Retailers

When purchasing holiday gifts this year, which 3 retailers will probably receive most of your spending? Choose up to 3.

Retailer	Likelihood
Amazon.com	64%
Walmart	62%
Target	44%
Kohl's	17%
Best Buy	10%
T.J. Maxx	9%
Bath & Body Works	9%
Costco	8%
Macy's	8%
Sam's Club	6%
Gamestop	6%

CHAPTER 15

MEDIA AND SOCIAL MEDIA

Source: eMarketer
Published: August 2019

Cord-cutting accelerates

Cord-cutting is when consumers stop paying for cable television and instead subscribe to internet streaming services. In 2019 pay TV households in the U.S. declined by 4.2%.

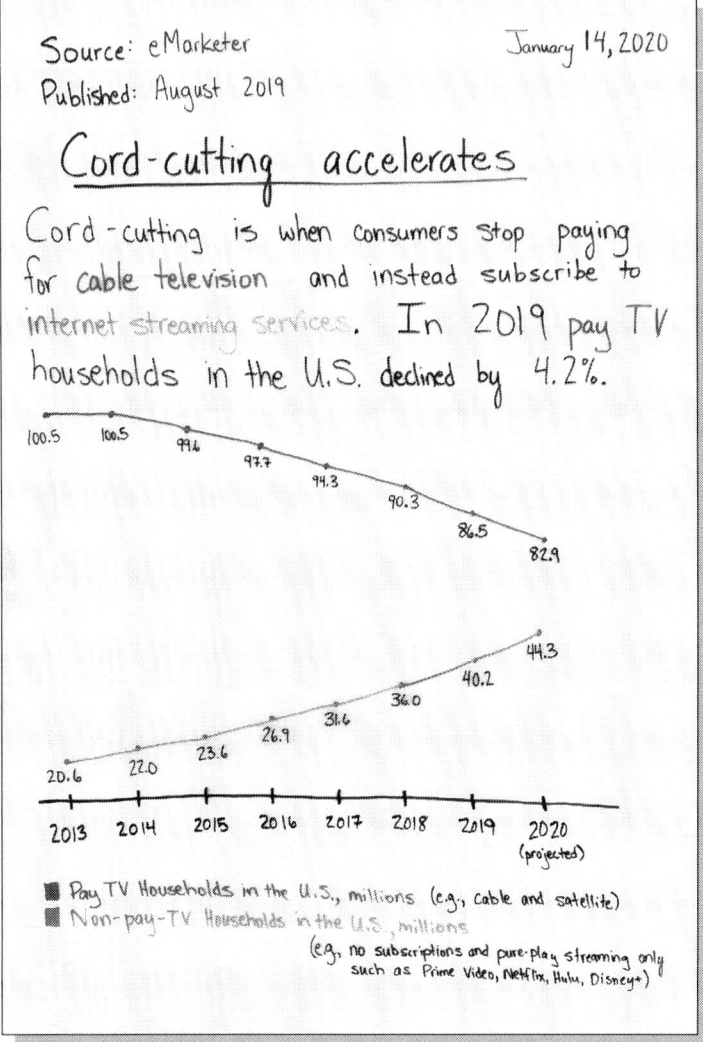

Pay TV Households in the U.S., millions (e.g., cable and satellite)

Non-pay-TV Households in the U.S., millions
(e.g., no subscriptions and pure-play streaming only such as Prime Video, Netflix, Hulu, Disney+)

Source: eMarketer
Published: August 2019

Cord-Cutting Accelerates

Cord-cutting is when consumers stop paying for cable television and instead subscribe to internet streaming services. In 2019 pay TV households in the U.S. declined by 4.2% to 86.5 million.

Year	Pay TV households in the US *in millions*	Non-Pay TV households in the US *in millions*
2013	100.5	20.6
2014	100.5	22.0
2015	99.6	23.6
2016	97.7	26.9
2017	94.3	31.6
2018	90.3	36.0
2019	86.5	40.2

Pay TV includes cable and satellite customers. Non-Pay-TV includes no subscription and pure-play streaming services such as Prime Video, Netflix, Hulu, and Disney+.

Source: Deloitte
Published: 2019

May 1

Consumers fatigued with video streaming services

69% of U.S. consumers have 1 or more Streaming video services

65% of U.S. consumers have a traditional pay T.V. subscription

In 2018, 57% of paid streaming consumers subscribe to access original content. Among millenials it's even higher at 71%.

47% of consumers are frustrated by the growing number of subscriptions they need → 300+ to piece together to watch what they want.

Source: Deloitte
Published: 2019

American Consumers Fatigued with Video Streaming Services

More consumers have at least one streaming video subscription (69%) than have a traditional pay TV subscription (65%).

In 2018, 57% of paid streaming video users said they subscribed to access original content. Among millennials, it's even higher at 71%.

47% of consumers are frustrated by the growing number of subscriptions they need to piece together to watch what they want.

Source: Nielsen
Published: February 2020

Streaming distribution by brand

Streaming continues to eat up a bigger chunk of viewers' time, though it's still outweighed by traditional TV. Among U.S. homes that are capable of over the internet streaming, 19% of their TV time was spent on streaming during Q4 2019. Within this streaming time:

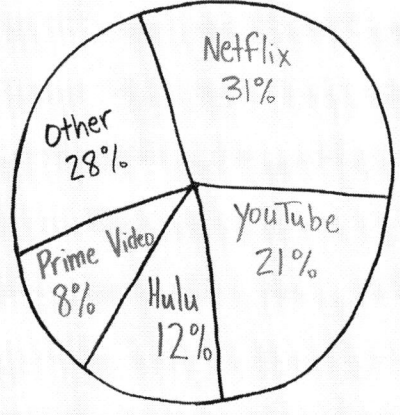

Netflix 31%

Other 28%

Prime Video 8%

Hulu 12%

YouTube 21%

Source: Nielsen
Published: February 2020

Streaming Distribution By Brand

Streaming continues to eat up a bigger chunk of viewers' time, though it's still outweighed by traditional TV. Among U.S. homes that are capable of over the internet streaming, 19% of their TV time was spent on streaming during the fourth quarter of 2019. Within this streaming time:

- Netflix 31%
- YouTube 21%
- Hulu 12%
- Prime Video 8%
- Other 28%

Source: Wikipedia
Published: September 2019

Prime Video wins big at the Emmys

An Emmy Award is an American award that recognizes excellence in the television industry. In just 5 years, the networks who won Major awards has shifted towards digital streaming companies. Major constitutes the categories of: Program, Acting, Directing, and Writing.

71st Emmy Awards	Network	Major Wins
2019 (Congratulations to the team!)	HBO	9
2019	. . . Prime Video	7
2019	Netflix	4
2019	FX	2
2019	NBC	2

66th Emmy Awards	Network	Major Wins
2014	AMC	5
2014	CBS	5
2014	FX	5
2014	HBO	4
2014	ABC	3
2014	PBS	3

Source: Wikipedia
Published: September 2019

Prime Video Wins Big at the Emmys

An Emmy Award is an American award that recognizes excellence in the television industry. In just 5 years, the networks who won Major awards has shifted towards digital streaming companies. Major constitutes the categories of: Program, Acting, Directing, and Writing.

71st Emmy Awards	Network	Major Wins
2019	HBO	9
2019	Prime Video	7
2019	Netflix	4
2019	FX	2
2019	NBC	2

66th Emmy Awards	Network	Major Wins
2014	AMC	5
2014	CBS	5
2014	FX	5
2014	HBO	4
2014	ABC	3
2014	PBS	3

Source: Rivaliq

Published: February 2019

n=1,000 companies

The lack of social interaction in social media

The majority of social media users spend time scrolling and consuming content with minimal social interactions.

Engagement rate is the liklihood of a person interacting with a post (e.g. like, comment, share).

Social Media	Engagement rate
Instagram	1.60%
Facebook	0.09%
Twitter	0.05%

Source: Rivaliq
Published: February 2019
n = 1,000 companies

The Lack of Social Interaction in Social Media

The majority of social media users spend time scrolling and consuming content with minimal social interactions. The engagement rate is the likelihood of a person interacting with a post (e.g., like, comment, share).

Engagement rate on popular social media platforms:

- 1.60% on Instagram
- 0.09% on Facebook
- 0.05% on Twitter

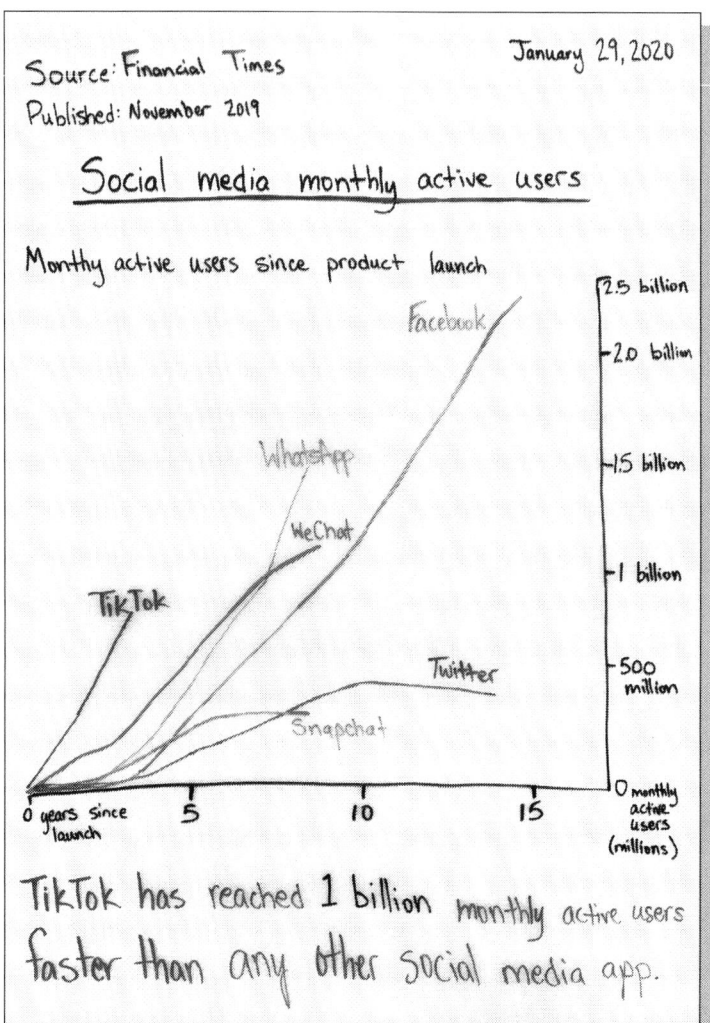

Source: Financial Times
Published: November 2019

January 29, 2020

Social media monthly active users

Monthly active users since product launch

- Facebook
- WhatsApp
- WeChat
- TikTok
- Twitter
- Snapchat

2.5 billion
2.0 billion
1.5 billion
1 billion
500 million
0 monthly active users (millions)

0 years since launch   5   10   15

TikTok has reached 1 billion monthly active users faster than any other social media app.

Source: Financial Times
Published: November 2019

Social Media Monthly Active Users

Social Media	Years After Launch	Monthly Active Users *in millions*
TikTok	3	1,000
WeChat	7	1,200
WhatsApp	8	1,500
Instagram	7	1,000
Snapchat	7	400
Twitter	13	400
Facebook	14	2,400

TikTok has reached 1 billion monthly active users faster than any other social media app.

Source: The CMO Survey   October 1

Published: February 2019

n = 323 top marketers at for-profit U.S. companies

How does your firm use social media?

Chief Marketing Officers (CMO) were asked to check all the uses of social media that apply to their business.

Use of social media	% of Respondents
Brand awareness and brand building	88.2%
Introducing new products and services	64.7
Acquiring new customers	60.1
Brand promotions	59.2
Retaining current customers	55.5
Improving customer service	40.8
Improving employee engagement	35.3
Marketing research	33.6
Identifying new customer groups you currently don't target	25.6
Identifying new product or service opportunities	17.2
Improving current products or services	13.9

Source: The CMO Survey
Published: February 2019
n = 323 top marketers at for-profit U.S. companies

How Does Your Firm Use Social Media?

Chief Marketing Officers were asked to check all the uses of social media that apply to their business.

Use of Social Media	% of Respondents
Brand awareness and brand building	88%
Introducing new products and services	65%
Acquiring new customers	60%
Brand promotions	59%
Retaining current customers	56%
Improving customer service	41%
Improving employee engagement	35%
Marketing research	34%
Identifying new customer groups you currently don't target	26%
Identifying new product and service opportunities	17%
Improving current products or services	14%

Source: National Research Group

Published: June 2019

n= 1,500 consumers

Fortnite: the new social media

In less than 2 years, Fortnite has attracted more than 250 million users around the world.

82% of its total audience is under 35 years old.

For ages 10-17 who play at least once a week, Fortnite is consuming 25% of their free time.

Entertainment service	% of Americans (ages 10-17) using weekly
YouTube	93%
Netflix	73
Instagram	56
Facebook	47
Snapchat	47
Hulu	43
Prime Video	43
Fortnite	40
Twitter	34

Bonus facts:

1) The biggest moment in Fortnite history was a Feb. 2019 concert w/ Marshmello drawing 10.7 million attendees.

2) Fortnite parent company Epic acquired social video app Houseparty yesterday.

Source: National Research Group
Published: June 2019
N = 1,500 consumers

Fortnite: The New Social Media

In less than two years, Fortnite has attracted more than 250 million users around the world. 82% of its total audience is under 35 years old. For ages 10–17 who play at least once a week, Fortnite is consuming 25% of their free time.

Entertainment Service	% of Americans (Ages 10-17) Using Weekly
YouTube	93%
Netflix	73%
Instagram	56%
Facebook	47%
Snapchat	47%
Hulu	43%
Prime Video	43%
Fortnite	40%
Twitter	34%
Candy Crush	30%
Twitch	24%
Steam	24%
Clash of Clans	20%
TikTok	17%

Bonus:

The biggest moment in Fortnite's history was in February 2019 when Marshmello hosted a virtual concert with 10.7 million people attending.

CHAPTER 16

DEVICES

Source: Common Sense Media   March 19, 2020
Published: May 2019
n= 500 U.S. parents and
   their children age 12-18

How mobile devices affect daily life

Parents and their children were surveyed in 2016
and 2019 to understand how mobile devices are
affecting families.

Devices come to bed with us.
   At night, 63% of parents and 39% of children
   keep their device within reach of the bed.

Sleep is being interrupted.
   36% of teens and 26% of parents wake up to check
   their mobile device at least once during the night.

Parents are increasingly concerned about their use.
   In 2016, 29% of parents said they think they spend
   "too much" time on their devices compared to
   52% of parents in 2019.

Devices distract us daily.
   In 2019, 54% of parents and 58% of teens
   felt distracted by their mobile device at least
   once a day.

Source: Common Sense Media
Published: May 2019
n = 500 U.S. parents and their children age 12-18

How mobile devices affect daily life

Parents and their children were surveyed in 2016 and 2019 to understand how mobile devices are affecting families.

Devices come to bed with us. At night, 63% of parents and 39% of children keep their device within reach of the bed.

Sleep is being interrupted. 36% of teens and 26% of parents wake up to check their mobile device at least once during the night.

Parents are increasingly concerned about their use. In 2016, 29% of parents said they think they spend "too much" time on their devices compared to 52% of parents in 2019.

Devices distract us daily. In 2019, 54% of parents and 58% of teens felt distracted by their mobile device at least once a day.

Source: Common Sense Media
Published: May 2019
n = 1,000 parents and children, U.S.

July 1

How devices affect daily life

% who wake up to check their mobile device during the night

Teens   36%
Parents 26%

% who feel addicted to their devices

Teens   39%
Parents 45%

% who think they spend too much time on their devices

Teens   39%
Parents 52%

Source: Common Sense Media
Published: May 2019
n = 1,000 parents and children, U.S.

How Devices (Phones and Tablets) Affect Daily Life

% who wake up to check their mobile device during the night:

- Teens *36%*
- Parents *26%*

% who feel addicted to their devices:

- Teens *39%*
- Parents *45%*

% who think they spend too much time on their devices:

- Teens *39%*
- Parents *52%*

Source: Statista
Published: May 2019

Mobile apps by the numbers

Most popular Apple App Store categories

Games	24.63% of apps
Business	9.76%
Education	8.52%
Lifestyle	8.33%
Entertainment	5.99%
Utilities	5.18%

App Stores - # of apps available

of apps

Store	# of apps
Google Play	2,100,000
Apple App Store	1,800,000
Windows Store	669,000
Amazon Appstore	475,000
Blackberry World	234,500

Source: Statista
Published: May 2019

Mobile Apps by the Numbers

Most popular Apple App Store categories:

- **Games** — 24.6%
- **Business** — 9.8%
- **Education** — 8.5%
- **Lifestyle** — 8.3%
- **Entertainment** — 6.0%
- **Utilities** — 5.2%
- **Travel** — 3.9%
- **Health & Fitness** — 3.0%
- **Food & Drink** — 2.9%

App Stores — Number of apps available:

- **Google Play** — 2,100,000
- **Apple App Store** — 1,800,000
- **Windows Store** — 669,000
- **Amazon Appstore** — 475,000
- **Blackberry World** — 234,500

Source: Statista   November 20, 2020
Published: October 2020

The Most Popular Social Networks

Approximately 3.6 billion internet users worldwide are using social networks. Ranked by the estimated number of active users, they are:

Social Network	Owner	Active users worldwide (as of October 2020)
Facebook	— Facebook →	2.7 billion
YouTube	— Google →	2.0 billion
WhatsApp	— Facebook →	2.0 billion
Facebook Messenger	— Facebook →	1.3 billion
WeChat	— Tencent →	1.2 billion
Instagram	— Facebook →	1.2 billion
TikTok	— ByteDance →	0.7 billion
QQ	— Tencent →	0.6 billion

Source: Statista
Published: October 2020

The Most Popular Social Networks

Approximately 3.6 billion internet users worldwide are using social networks. Ranked by the estimated number of active users, they are:

Social Network	Owner	Active users worldwide *as of October 2020*
Facebook	Facebook	2.7 billion
YouTube	Google	2.0 billion
WhatsApp	Facebook	2.0 billion
Facebook Messenger	Facebook	1.3 billion
WeChat	Tencent	1.2 billion
Instagram	Facebook	1.2 billion
TikTok	ByteDance	0.7 billion
QQ	Tencent	0.6 billion

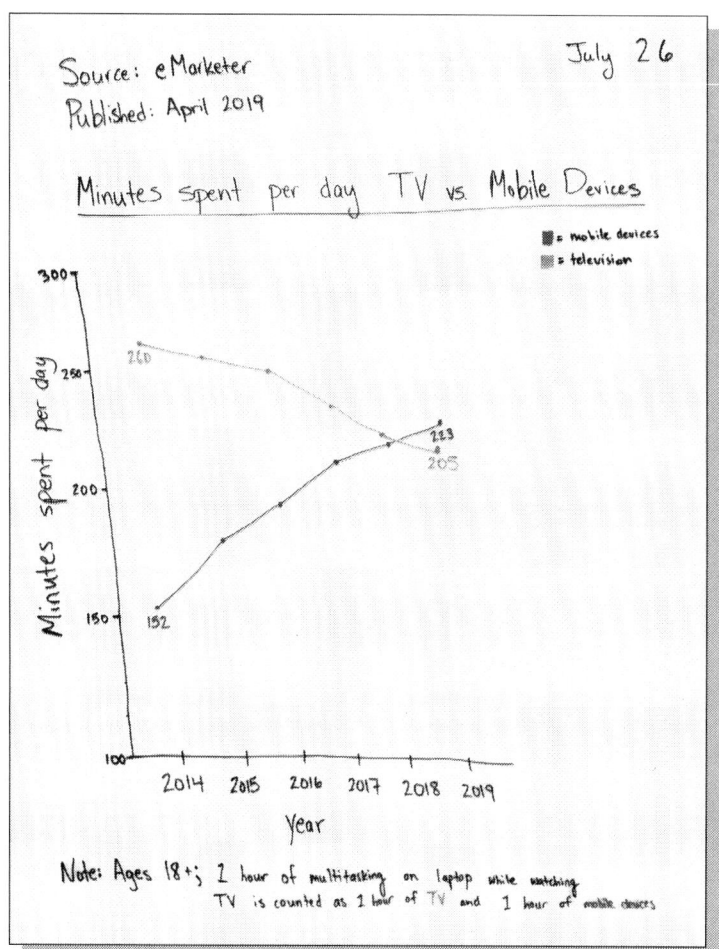

Source: eMarketer
Published: April 2019

July 26

Minutes spent per day TV vs. Mobile Devices

■ = mobile devices
■ = television

Minutes spent per day (y-axis)
300
250 — 260
200
150 — 152
100

Year (x-axis): 2014 2015 2016 2017 2018 2019

213
205

Note: Ages 18+; 2 hour of multitasking on laptop while watching TV is counted as 1 hour of TV and 1 hour of mobile devices

Source: eMarketer
Published: April 2019

Minutes Spent Per Day TV vs. Mobile Devices

Year	TV in minutes	Mobile Devices in minutes
2014	260	152
2015	250	169
2016	245	188
2017	226	205
2018	214	215
2019	205	223

Note: Ages 18+; 1 hour of multitasking on laptop while watching TV is counted as 1 hour for TV and 1 hour for laptop.

Source: Qustodio
Published: May 2020
n= 60,000 families with children

July 1, 2020

Kids' app habit insights

Research conducted in 2019 and 2020 in the US, UK, and Spain sought to share insights on children's screen-time habits. Here are the key takeaways across four app categories:

online video, social media, video games, and education for children ages 4 to 15.

1. YouTube is the most popular source of online videos for kids (despite being for ages 13+)

2. TikTok drove the growth of social app use by 200% in 2020.

3. Kids spend 85 minutes per day on YouTube. (100 minutes in the US)

4. Kids spend 80 minutes per day on TikTok.

5. Kids spend 60 minutes per day playing video games.

6. Google Classroom is used by 65% of children in Spain.

Source: Qustodio
Published: May 2020
n = 60,000 families with children

Kids' App Habit Insights

Research conducted in 2019 and 2020 in the US, UK, and Spain sought to share insights on children's screen-time habits. Here are the key takeaways across four app categories: online video, social media, video games, and education for children ages 4 to 15.

1. YouTube is the most popular source of online videos for kids (despite being for ages 13+)
2. TikTok drove the growth of social app use up by 200% in 2020.
3. Kids spend 85 minutes per day on YouTube. (100 minutes per day in the US)
4. Kids spend 80 minutes per day on TikTok.
5. Kids spend 60 minutes per day playing video games.
6. Google Classroom is used by 65% of children in Spain.

Source: Pew Research   October 21, 2020
Published: July 2020
n = 3,640 US parents

Parenting Children in the Age of Screens

Parenting has never been easy. But the widespread adoption of smartphones and the rise of social media has introduced a new wrinkle to the challenges of parenthood.

When US parents with a child age 5 to 11 were asked about their child's digital use, they said:

Parents say they...	Percent of Parents
Limit the time of day or length of time a child can use screens	86%
Take away the child's phone or internet privileges as punishment	80%
Check the websites or apps their child visits or uses	75%
Use parental controls to restrict screen time	72%
Look at the child's phone calls or text messages	49%
Track their child's location	33%
Friend or follow the child on social media	28%

Source: Pew Research
Published: July 2020
n = 3,640 U.S. Parents

Parenting Children in the Age of Screens

Parenting has never been easy. But the widespread adoption of smartphones and the rise of social media has introduced a new wrinkle to the challenges of parenthood.

When U.S. parents with a child age 5 to 11 were asked about their child's digital use:

Parents say they...	Percent of Parents
Limit the time of day or length of time a child can use screens	86%
Take away the child's phone or internet privileges as punishment	80%
Check the websites or apps their child visits or uses	75%
Use parental controls to restrict screen time	72%
Look at the child's phone calls or text messages	49%
Track their child's location	33%
Friend or follow the child on social media	28%

Source: App Annie
Published: January 2020

The state of mobile

Macro-trends for mobile devices in 2019:

- 204 billion worldwide app downloads (+6% YoY)
- $120 billion worldwide app store consumer spend
- Games make up 72% of app store spend
- 3.7 hours per day spent in mobile apps by the average Android user (iOS data unavailable)
- $190 billion mobile advertising spend by brands

Top apps: Worldwide monthly active users

1.	Whatsapp Messenger	Facebook
2.	Facebook	Facebook
3.	Facebook Messenger	Facebook
4.	WeChat	Tencent
5.	Instagram	Facebook
6.	TikTok	ByteDance
7.	Alipay	Ant Financial
8.	QQ	Tencent
9.	Taobao	Alibaba Group
10.	Baidu	Baidu

Source: App Annie
Published: January 2020

The State of Mobile

Macro-trends for mobile devices in 2019:

- *204 billion* worldwide app downloads (*+6% YoY*).
- *$120 billion* worldwide app store consumer spend.
- Games make up *72%* of app store spend.
- *3.7 hours* per day spent in mobile apps by the average Android user (iOS data unavailable).
- *$190 billion* mobile advertising spend by brands.

Top Apps: Worldwide Monthly Active Users

1. WhatsApp Messenger — Facebook
2. Facebook — Facebook
3. Facebook Messenger — Facebook
4. WeChat — Tencent
5. Instagram — Facebook
6. TikTok — ByteDance
7. Alipay — Ant Financial
8. QQ — Tencent
9. Taobao — Alibaba Group
10. Baidu — Baidu

Source: Cornerstone Advisors June 12
Published: Q2 2019
n = 2,506 U.S. customers

Merchant apps on U.S. consumers' smartphones

of mobile app customers
(in millions)

Merchant	# of mobile app customers (in millions)
Walmart	58.5
Amazon	54.4
Uber	52.1
Starbucks	44.2
CVS	28.2
Kohl's	24.1
Chik-Fil-A	23.4
Panera	18.7
Wendy's	15.1

Source: Cornerstone Advisors
Published: Q2 2019
N = 2,506 U.S. consumers

Merchant Apps on U.S. Consumers' Smartphones

Merchant	# of mobile app customers (in millions)
Walmart	58.5
Amazon	54.4
Uber	52.1
Starbucks	44.2
CVS	28.2
Kohl's	24.1
Chik-Fil-A	23.4
Dunkin' Donuts	21.6
Panera	18.7
Wendy's	15.1

Source: NPR
Published: Jan 2019
n= 1,002 telephone respondents

Smart Speaker Report

21% of people in the U.S. 18+ own a smart speaker, or around 53 million people.

In the 2018 holiday season, 8% of people in the U.S. got a smart speaker.

There were 14 million new smart speaker owners in 2018.

Awareness of smart speaker

Jan. 2016	62%
Dec. 2017	75
Dec. 2018	77

Source: NPR
Published: January 2019
n = 1,002 telephone respondents

The Smart Speaker Report

21% of people in the U.S. 18+ own a Smart Speaker, or around *53 million* people. In the 2018 holiday season, *8%* of people in the U.S. got a smart speaker. There were *14 million* new smart speaker owners in 2018.

Awareness of "smart speakers":

- *Jan 2016–62%*
- *December 2017–75%*
- *December 2018–77%*

SECTION 4

THINK BIG

CHAPTER 17

THE INTERNET AND WORLD WIDE WEB

Source: Our World in Data
Published: April 2019

December 6

The Internet's history

1965: The first email system MAILBOX was used at MIT

1972: Email is invented allowing for messages between computers

1989: World Wide Web created

1991: First web page published

1994: Netscape web browser released

1995: eBay, Yahoo!, and Amazon.com

1997: Google search

1999: Alibaba and Napster

2001: Wikipedia

2004: Facebook

2005: YouTube and Google Maps

2007: iPhone

2008: Github and Chrome browser

2009: Whatsapp, Uber, Bitcoin, Blockchain

2010: Instagram

2011: WeChat and Siri

2014: Amazon Alexa

2018: EU's General Data Protection Regulation (GDPR)

Source: Our World in Data
Published: April 2019

The Internet's History

- **1965:** the first email system MAILBOX was used at MIT
- **1972:** Email is invented allowing for messages between computers
- **1989:** World Wide Web created
- **1991:** First web page published
- **1994:** Netscape web browser released
- **1995:** eBay, Yahoo, and Amazon.com
- **1997:** Google search
- **1999:** Alibaba and Napster
- **2001:** Wikipedia
- **2004:** Facebook
- **2005:** YouTube and Google Maps
- **2007:** iPhone
- **2008:** Github and Chrome browser
- **2009:** Whatsapp, Uber, Bitcoin, Blockchain
- **2010:** Instagram
- **2011:** WeChat and Siri
- **2014:** Amazon Alexa
- **2018:** EU's General Data Protection Regulation (GDPR)

Source: Internet World Stats

Published: June 2019

July 31

World Internet Usage and Population

☐ = Internet Users   ☐ = Non internet users

Asia   52% [=====================================]

Africa   40% [==========]

Europe   87% [=====]

Latin America/ 68% [====]
Caribbean

North America 89% [==]

Middle East 67% [=]

Oceania /
Australia   68% ▮

```
  0      1B      2B      3B      4B
```

Population

Source: Internet World Stats
Published: June 2019

World Internet Usage and Population Statistics

World Regions	Population (2019 estimate)	Population (% of world)	Internet User (% of population)	Non Internet User (% of population)
Africa	1.3 billion	17%	40%	60%
Asia	4.2 billion	55%	52%	48%
Europe	829.2 million	11%	87%	13%
Latin America/ Caribbean	658.3 million	9%	68%	32%
Middle East	258.4 million	3%	67%	33%
North America	366.5 million	5%	89%	11%
Oceania/ Australia	41.8 million	1%	68%	32%
WORLD TOTAL	**7.7 billion**			

Source: Statista

Published: November 2019

December 15, 2020

Global internet users

The number of internet users is growing as more people have access to desktop computers, smartphones, and tablets.

Year	Number of internet users in billions (rounded)	Difference %
2005	1.1	N/A
2006	1.2	11%
2007	1.4	14%
2008	1.6	14%
2009	1.8	13%
2010	2.0	15%
2011	2.2	10%
2012	2.5	11%
2013	2.7	8%
2014	2.9	7%
2015	3.1	7%
2016	3.3	9%
2017	3.7	11%
2018	3.9	6%
2019	4.1	5%

Source: Statista
Published: November 2019

Global internet users

The number of internet users is growing as more people have access to desktop computers, smartphones, and tablets.

Year	Number of internet users in billions (rounded)	Difference %
2005	1.1	N/A
2006	1.2	11%
2007	1.4	14%
2008	1.6	14%
2009	1.8	13%
2010	2.0	15%
2011	2.2	10%
2012	2.5	11%
2013	2.7	8%
2014	2.9	7%
2015	3.1	7%
2016	3.3	9%
2017	3.7	11%
2018	3.9	6%
2019	4.1	5%

Source: Internet World Stats   August 18, 2020
Published: June 2020

Growth of the internet

Interviewer: What propelled you to say "I'm quitting my job at a hedge fund (DE Shaw) and I'm going to start a company selling books via the internet?"

°°(We love facts!)

"In 1994 I came across the fact that the worldwide web was growing at 2,300% a year. Anything growing that fast is going to be big. I decided to come up with a business idea where the internet could grow around it. I picked books because there are more items in the books category than any other category." — Jeff Bezos

Internet adoption over the last 25 years

Date	Number of Users	% World Population
December 1995	16 million	0.4 %
December 1997	70 million	1.7
December 1999	248 million	4.1
August 2001	513 million	8.6
December 2003	719 million	11.1
December 2005	1.02 billion	15.7
December 2007	1.32 billion	20.0
December 2009	1.80 billion	26.6
December 2011	2.27 billion	32.7
December 2013	2.80 billion	39.0
December 2015	3.37 billion	46.4
December 2017	4.16 billion	54.4
June 2020	4.65 billion	59.6

Source: Internet World Stats
Published: June 2020

Growth of the internet

Interviewer: "What propelled you to say I'm quitting my job at a hedge fund (DE Shaw) and I'm going to start a company selling books via the internet?"

"In 1994 I came across the fact that the world wide web was growing at 2,300% a year. Anything growing that fast is going to be big. I decided to come up with a business idea where the internet could grow around it. I picked books because there are more items in the books category than any other category."

—**Jeff Bezos**

Internet adoption over the last 25 years

Date	Number of Users	% World Population
December 1995	16 million	0.4%
December 1997	70 million	1.7%
December 1999	248 million	4.1%
August 2001	513 million	8.6%
December 2003	719 million	11.1%
December 2005	1.02 billion	15.7%
December 2007	1.32 billion	20.0%
December 2009	1.80 billion	26.6%
December 2011	2.27 billion	32.7%
December 2013	2.80 billion	39.0%
December 2015	3.37 billion	46.4%
December 2017	4.16 billion	54.4%
June 2020	4.65 billion	59.6%

Source: Statista
Published: February 2019

Internet users by country

This statistic shows users in selected countries in 2018 who accessed the internet via any device (i.e., Computers, mobile phones, tablets) at least once per month.

Countries	Internet users (millions)
China	805
India	483
United States	275
Brazil	138
Japan	118
Russia	117
Indonesia	95
Nigeria	92
Mexico	86
Germany	77
Philippines	70
United Kingdom	65
Vietnam	55
France	55
Turkey	54
South Korea	48
Thailand	41
Spain	41
Italy	38
South Africa	37

Source: Statista
Published: February 2019

Internet Users by Country

This statistic shows users in selected countries in 2018 who accessed the internet via any device (i.e., computers, mobile phones, and tablets) at least once per month.

After this fact was published, readers sent in questions with a common theme "What percentage of each country's population does this represent? The answer is 98% for the United Kingdom, 93% for Japan, and 93% for South Korea. At the bottom of the list, opportunity for adoption is greatest in Indonesia (35%) and India (36%).

Country	Internet Users (millions)	Population (millions)	% of Population as Internet Users
United Kingdom	65	66	98%
Japan	118	127	93%
Germany	77	83	93%
South Korea	48	52	92%
Spain	41	47	87%
United States	275	327	84%
France	55	67	82%
Russia	117	145	81%
Mexico	86	126	68%
Brazil	138	209	66%
Turkey	54	82	66%
Philippines	70	107	65%
South Africa	37	58	64%
Italy	38	60	63%
Thailand	41	69	59%
Vietnam	55	95	58%
China	805	1393	58%
Nigeria	92	196	47%
India	483	1353	36%
Indonesia	95	268	35%

Source: Statista
Published: May 2019

Languages of internet users

In 2019 there were 4.1 billion internet users worldwide. The most popular language, as measured by total users on the internet, is English, representing 25% of worldwide internet users, followed by Chinese with a 19% share.

Language	Percent of internet users
English	25
Chinese	19
Spanish	8
Arabic	5
Portugese	4
Indonesian / Malaysian	4
French	3
Japanese	3
Russian	3
German	2
Rest of languages	24

Source: Statista
Published: May 2019

Languages of Internet Users

In 2019 there were 4.1 billion internet users worldwide. The most popular language, as measured by total users on the internet, is English, representing 25% of worldwide internet users, followed by Chinese with a 19% share.

Language	Percent of Internet Users
English	25
Chinese	19
Spanish	8
Arabic	5
Portuguese	4
Indonesian / Malaysian	4
French	3
Japanese	3
Russian	3
German	2
Rest of languages	24

Source: TeleGeography and NEC
Published: March 2019

The backbone of the Internet

In 1858 a 4,000 kilometer (2,500 mile) long and 1.5 centimeter (0.6 inches) wide cable linked Europe and North America by telegraph.

U.S. President James Buchanan hailed the effort as a

"triumph more glorious than was ever won by conquer on the field of battle."

Undersea cables are the backbone of the Internet today:

- 99% of all international data is transmitted via undersea cables.

- The cable between Japan and the U.S. is 8,000 meters (5 miles) below sea level.
  That's the height of Mount Everest!

- Today there are around 380 undersea cables in operation around the world.

- Cables were traditionally owned by telecom carriers. In recent years Big Tech became major investors:

Google	7 cable investments
Microsoft	4
Facebook	3
Amazon	1

Source: TeleGeography and NEC
Published: March 2019

The Backbone of the Internet

In 1858 a 4,000 kilometer (2,500 mile) long and 1.5 centimeter (0.6 inch) wide cable linked Europe and North America by telegraph. U.S. President James Buchanan hailed the effort as a "triumph more glorious than was ever won by conquerors on the field of battle". (CNN)

Undersea cables are the backbone of the Internet today:

- 99% of all international data is transmitted via undersea cables.
- The cable between Japan and the U.S. is 8,000 meters (5 miles) below sea level. That's the height of Mount Everest!
- Today there are around 380 undersea cables in operation around the world.
- Cables were traditionally owned by telecom carriers. In recent years Big Tech became major investors:
  - **Google** — 7 cable investments
  - **Microsoft** — 4 cable investments
  - **Facebook** — 3 cable investments
  - **Amazon** — 1 cable investment

Source: Similar Web
Published: August 2019

Top Websites by traffic, worldwide

	URL*	Description	Monthly visits (in billions)
1	google.com	search	60.5
2	youtube.com	video	24.3
3	facebook.com	social	20.0
4	baidu.com	search	9.8
5	wikipedia.com	encyclopedia	4.7
6	twitter.com	social	3.9
7	yahoo.com	news, social, email	3.7
8	pornhub.com	pornography	3.3
9	instagram.com	pictures	3.2
10	xvideos.com	pornography	3.2
11	yandex.ru	search	3.1
12	ampproject.org	mobile pages	2.8
13	xnxx.com	pornography	2.5
14	amazon.com	shopping	2.4
15	live.com	email	2.3
16	vk.com	social	2.2
17	netflix.com	video	1.8
18	qq.com	messaging	1.8
19	whatsapp.com	messaging	1.8
20	mail.ru	email	1.6

*Traffic from web browsers, not mobile apps.

Source: Similar Web via Visual Capitalist
Published: August 2019

Top Websites by Traffic, Worldwide

	URL*	Description	Monthly visits (in billions)
1	google.com	search	60.5
2	youtube.com	video	24.3
3	facebook.com	social	20.0
4	baidu.com	search	9.8
5	wikipedia.com	encyclopedia	4.7
6	twitter.com	social	3.9
7	yahoo.com	news, email, search	3.7
8	pornhub.com	pornography	3.3
9	instagram.com	pictures	3.2
10	xvideos.com	pornography	3.2
11	yandex.ru	search	3.1
12	ampproject.org	mobile pages	2.8
13	xnxx.com	pornography	2.5
14	amazon.com	shopping	2.4
15	live.com	email	2.3
16	vk.com	social	2.2
17	netflix.com	video	1.8
18	qq.com	messaging	1.8
19	whatsapp.com	messaging	1.8
20	mail.ru	email	1.6

*traffic is from web browsers, not mobile apps.

Source: W3Counter
Published: May 2020

May 19, 2020

Web browser market share

Browser family usage share

Browser	April 2008	April 2014	April 2020
Internet Explorer and Edge	63%	18%	7%
Firefox	30%	19%	5%
Chrome	0%	37%	62%
Safari	3%	17%	12%
Opera	2%	3%	3%
Other	2%	6%	11%

Most popular screen resolutions

Resolution (pixels)	Share
640 x 360	16%
1366 x 768	11%
1920 x 1080	6%
760 x 360	5%
1024 x 768	5%

Source: W3Counter
Published: May 2020

Web Browser Market Share

Browser family usage share

Browser	April 2008	April 2004	April 2020
Internet Explorer & Edge	63%	18%	7%
Firefox	30%	19%	5%
Chrome	0%	37%	62%
Safari	3%	17%	12%
Opera	2%	3%	3%
Other	2%	6%	11%

Most popular screen resolutions

Resolution (pixels)	Share
640x360	16%
1366x768	11%
1920x1080	6%
760x360	6%
1024x768	5%

While 640x360 pixels is the most common, this can be a bit confusing as a device can display a multiple of the declared pixel value. For example, 360x640 pixels at 300% DPI is 1080x1920 - which is the 1080p standard - yet would register as 640x360 in the table above

Source: Jeff Bezos, TED Talk   March 6, 2020
Published: February 2003

The electricity metaphor for the web's future

Folks compared the dot-com bubble in the late 1990s with the gold rush of 1848 - 1855. This analogy is weak because while gold has a limited supply, innovation is without end.

A better analogy is the Internet and the electric industry. Both are horizontal enabling layers that span across industries. The killer app that got the world ready for wired appliances was the light bulb. Instead of putting electricity into the home, people viewed it as putting lighting into the home. Each room typically had a light socket where you'd unscrew the light bulb and screw in an appliance when you wanted to use it. There was no off button, you'd simply unscrew the appliance when done using it.

"If you really do believe it's the very, very beginning of the Internet, then you're incredibly optimistic. I do believe there is more innovation ahead of us than behind us."
                    — Jeff Bezos

Source: Jeff Bezos, TED Talk
Published: February 2003

The Electricity Metaphor for the Web's Future

Folks compared the dot-com bubble in the late 1990s with the gold rush of 1848-1855. This analogy is weak because while gold has a limited supply, innovation is without end.

A better analogy is the Internet and the electric industry. Both are horizontal enabling layers that span across industries. The killer app that got the world ready for wired appliances was the light bulb. Instead of putting electricity into the home, people viewed it as putting lighting into the home. Each room typically had a light socket where you'd unscrew the light bulb and screw in an appliance when you wanted to use it. There was no off button, you'd simply unscrew the appliance when done using it.

"If you really do believe it's the very, very beginning of the Internet, then you're incredibly optimistic. I do believe there is more innovation ahead of us than behind us."

—**Jeff Bezos**

Source: Bill Gates
Published: May 1995

February 20, 2020

The Internet Tidal Wave

25 years ago Bill Gates sent a 9-page memo to the Executive Staff at Microsoft about the Internet. Highlights:

· I have gone through several stages of increasing my views of the Internet's importance. Now I assign the Internet the highest level of importance; the Internet is crucial to every part of our business.

· The Internet is the most important single development to come along since the IBM PC was introduced in 1981.

· I think that virtually every PC will be used to connect to the Internet.

· The amount of free information available today on the Internet is quite amazing.

· The Internet is a tidal wave. It changes the rules. It is an incredible opportunity as well as incredible challenge.

· I encourage everyone on the Executive Staff and their direct reports to use the Internet.

Source: Bill Gates
Published: May 1995

The Internet Tidal Wave

25 years ago, Bill Gates sent a 9-page memo to the Executive Staff at Microsoft about the Internet.

Highlights:

- I have gone through several stages of increasing my views of the Internet's importance. Now I assign the Internet the highest level of importance; the Internet is crucial to every part of our business.
- The Internet is the most important single development to come along since the IBM PC was introduced in 1981.
- I think that virtually every PC will be used to connect to the Internet.
- The amount of free information available today on the Internet is quite amazing.
- The Internet is a tidal wave. It changes the rules. It is an incredible opportunity as well as an incredible challenge.
- I encourage everyone on the executive staff and their direct reports to use the Internet.

Source: AMZN Letter to shareholders   January 23, 2020
Published: April 2008

<u>Information snacking</u>

"Lately, networked tools such as desktop computers, laptops, and cell phones have changed us.

They've shifted us more toward information snacking and toward shorter attention spans. I value my BlackBerry — I'm convinced it makes me more productive — but I don't want to read a three-hundred-page document on it. If our tools make information snacking easier, we'll shift more toward information snacking and away from long-form reading.

Kindle is purpose-built for long-form reading. We hope Kindle and its successors move us into a world with longer spans of attention, providing a counterbalance to the recent proliferation of info-snacking tools. We're hoping that Kindle will "start a fire" and improve the world of reading."

— Jeff Bezos

Source: AMZN Letter to shareholders
Published: April 2008

Information Snacking

"Lately, networked tools such as desktop computers, laptops, and cell phones have changed us. They've shifted us more toward **information snacking** and toward shorter attention spans. I value my BlackBerry — I'm convinced it makes me more productive — but I don't want to read a three-hundred-page document on it. If our tools make **information snacking** easier, we'll shift more toward **information snacking** and away from long-form reading.

Kindle is purpose-built for long-form reading. We hope Kindle and its successors move us into a world with longer spans of attention, providing a counterbalance to the recent proliferation of **info-snacking** tools. We're hopeful that Kindle will "start a fire" and improve the world of reading."

—Jeff Bezos

Source: Shervin Pishevar   November 3, 2020
Published: October 2020

Big things start small

While Amazon, Apple, Microsoft, and Alphabet
(Google's parent company) are all among the largest
technology companies today, they all began as
startups. Looking back at old business cards from
Jeff, Steve, Bill, and Larry bring a sense of nostalgia.
Big things truly do start small.

Source: Shervin Pishevar
Published: October 2020

Big things start small

While Amazon, Apple, Microsoft, and Alphabet (Google's parent company) are all among the largest technology companies today, they all began as startups. Looking back at old business cards from Jeff, Steve, Bill, and Larry bring a sense of nostalgia. Big things truly do start small.

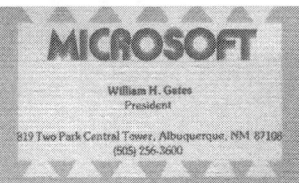

Source: Princeton
Published: June 2010

In the end, we are our choices

Jeff Bezos delivered the graduation speech to Princeton University's Class of 2010. Bezos graduated from Princeton in 1986 with a degree in computer science and electrical engineering.

Highlights from his 13-minute speech:

- Bezos got the idea to start Amazon when he came across the fact that Web usage was growing at 2,300% per year. He had never seen or heard of anything growing that fast.

We love facts!

- It is harder to be kind than clever. Cleverness is a gift while being kind to others is a choice.

  ↳ Gifts are easy; they're given after all. Choices are hard.

  ↳ One's character is reflected not in the gifts one is endowed with at birth (e.g., intelligence, creativity) but rather by the choices one makes over the course of a lifetime.

- When you are 80 years old and in a quiet moment of reflection, narrating for only yourself the most personal version of your life story, the telling that will be most compact and meaningful will be the series of choices you've made.

In the end, we are our choices.
Build yourself a great story.

Source: Princeton
Published: June 2010

In the end, we are our choices

Jeff Bezos delivered the graduation speech to Princeton University's Class of 2010. Bezos graduated from Princeton in 1986 with a degree in computer science and electrical engineering.

Highlights from his 13-minute speech:

- Bezos got the idea to start Amazon when he came across the fact that Web usage was growing at 2,300% per year. He had never seen or heard of anything that grew that fast.
- It is harder to be kind than clever. Cleverness is a gift while being kind to others is a choice.
  - Gifts are easy; they're given after all. Choices are hard.
  - One's character is reflected not in the gifts one is endowed with at birth (e.g., intelligence, creativity) but rather by the choices one makes over the course of a lifetime.
- When you are 80 years old and in a quiet moment of reflection, narrating for only yourself the most personal version of your life story, the telling that will be most compact and meaningful will be the series of choices you've made.

In the end, we are our choices. Build yourself a great story.

Source: David Rubenstein
Published: September 2018

The power of wandering

" I believe in the power of wandering. All of the best decisions in business and my life have been made with heart, intuition, guts - not analysis. When you can make a decision with analysis, you should do so. But it turns out that your most important choices in life are made with instinct, taste, and heart. "

- Jeff Bezos

An example: The Washington Post

Jeff's decision-making process to purchase the WaPo for $250 million was intuition, not analysis.

"The financials were upside down in 2013!
If this were a salty snack food company, my answer would have been no.
However, I decided that this is an institution important for democracy. I know when I'm 90, it will be one of the decisions I'm most proud of."

Source: David Rubenstein
Published: September 2018

The power of wandering

"I believe in the power of wandering. All of my best decisions in business and my life have been made with heart, intuition, guts — not analysis. When you can make a decision with analysis, you should do so. But it turns out that your most important choices in life are made with instinct, taste, and heart."

— Jeff Bezos

An example: *The Washington Post*

Jeff's decision-making process to purchase *The Washington Post* for $250 million was intuition, not analysis.

"The financials were upside down in 2013! If this were a salty snack food company, my answer would have been no. However, I decided that this is an institution important for democracy. I know that when I'm 90, it will be one of the decisions I'm most proud of."

Source: Computer History Museum   November 2, 2020
Published: circa 1980

A bicycle for our minds

"I read a study that measured the efficiency of locomotion for various species on the planet by measuring the energy required to move a kilometer. The condor [a species of bird] won as it used the least energy to fly a kilometer; humans [had] a rather unimpressive showing.

But fortunately, someone was insightful enough to test a human on a bicycle, which blew the condor off the charts!

This shows that humans are tool makers that can amplify their abilities. And that's what a computer is to me. A computer is the most remarkable tool that we've ever come up with, and it's the equivalent of a bicycle for our minds."

-Steve Jobs

Source: Computer History Museum
Published: circa 1980

A bicycle for our minds

"I read a study that measured the efficiency of locomotion for various species on the planet by measuring the energy required to move a kilometer. The condor [a species of bird] won as it used the least energy to fly a kilometer; humans [had] a rather unimpressive showing.

But fortunately, someone was insightful enough to test a human on a bicycle, which blew the condor off the charts!

This shows that **humans are tool makers that can amplify their abilities**. And that's what a computer is to me. A computer is the most remarkable tool that we've ever come up with, and it's the equivalent of a bicycle for our minds."

—**Steve Jobs**

CHAPTER 18

GLOBAL THINKING

Source: Britannica

Published: March 2019

November 12, 2020

The History of Technology

Technology is the application of scientific knowledge for practical purposes. Highlights in technological advancements over the past 1,000 years include:

- 1044 – magnetic compass
- 1455 – printing press
- 1765 – steam engine
- 1827 – photography
- 1844 – telegraph
- 1879 – electric light (Thomas Edison)
- 1885 – automobile
- 1901 – radio
- 1903 – airplane (Wright brothers)
- 1942 – nuclear power (Manhattan Project)
- 1947 – the transistor
- 1974 – personal computer (Altair)
- 1974 – the internet (TCP/IP)
- 2012 – CRISPR (a method for editing genes)

Source: Britannica
Published: March 2019

The History of Technology

Technology is the application of scientific knowledge for practical purposes. Highlights in technological advancements over the past 1,000 years include:

- 1044 – magnetic compass
- 1455 – printing press
- 1765 – steam engine
- 1827 – photography
- 1844 – telegraph
- 1879 – electric light
- 1885 – automobile
- 1901 – radio
- 1903 – airplane
- 1942 – nuclear power
- 1947 – the transistor
- 1974 – personal computer
- 1974 – the internet
- 2012 – CRISPR

Source: Saamir Ansari

Published: July 2020

August 6, 2020

The worst year in history

2020 is one of the bleakest years in a generation. However, when speaking of the worst year recorded in human history, scholars and researchers agree on 536 AD.

- That year, a massive volcanic eruption choked the atmosphere with ash.

- Darkness loomed 24 hours/day for 2 years.

- Global temperatures plummeted, spawning the coldest decade in 2,000 years.

- Crops failed worldwide, and famine was rampant, ushering Europe into five centuries of economic, cultural, and demographic decline, a period historians call the Dark Ages.

Source: Saamir Ansari
Published: July 2020

The worst year in history

2020 is one of the bleakest years in a generation. However, when speaking of the worst year recorded in human history, scholars and researchers agree on 536 AD.

- That year, a massive volcanic eruption choked the atmosphere with ash.
- Darkness loomed 24 hours a day, for two years.
- Global temperatures plummeted, spawning the coldest decade in 2,000 years.
- Crops failed worldwide, and famine was rampant, ushering Europe into five centuries of economic, cultural, and demographic decline, a period historians call the "*Dark Ages.*"

Source: Our World in Data   June 21
Published: May 2019

A peak in world population

The most populated countries:
- (1) China   1.42 billion
- (2) India   1.37 billion
- (3) United States   329 million
- (4) Indonesia   269 million
- (5) Brazil   212 million

The United Nations projects that world population will peak at 11 billion people by 2100. At that time, 8 out of 10 people in the world will live in Asia or Africa.

Source: Our World in Data
Published: May 2019

A Peak in World Population

Largest countries today:

- China (1.42 billion)
- India (1.37 billion)
- United States (329 million)
- Indonesia (269 million)
- Brazil (212 million)

The United Nations projects that world population will peak at *11 billion* people by 2100. At that time, 8 out of 10 people in the world will live in Asia or Africa.

Source: Our World in Data
Published: May 2019

The most populous country

China has been the world's most populous country for a long time: back in 1750, it had a population of 225 million which was 28% of the world population.

By 2016 China grew to 1.4 billion, or 19% of the world population.

According to the United Nation's Population Division, by 2024 India is projected to surpass China to become the world's most populous country.

Source: Our World in Data
Published: May 2019

The Most Populous Country

China has been the world's most populous country for a long time: back in 1750, it had a population of *225 million* which was *28%* of the world population. By 2016, China had a population larger than *1.4 billion*.

According to the United Nation's Population Division, by 2024 India is projected to surpass China to become the world's most populous country.

Death by risk factor

The researchers examined the total number of deaths by risk factor, measured across all age groups and both sexes. The objective of the study is to better understand the changing health challenges being faced by people across the world.

Rank	Risk Factor	Number of Deaths (annual, in millions)
1	High blood pressure	10.4
2	Smoking (tobacco)	7.1
3	High blood sugar	6.5
4	Air pollution	4.9
5	Obesity	4.7
6	Alcohol use	2.8
7	Diet low in fruits	2.4
8	Diet low in vegetables	1.5
9	Low physical activity	1.3
10	Unsafe water source	1.2

Source: University of Washington
Published: November 2019

Deaths By Risk Factor

The researchers examined the total annual number of deaths by risk factor, measured across all age groups and both sexes. The objective of the study is to better understand the changing health challenges being faced by people across the world.

Rank	Risk Factor	Number of Deaths annual, in millions
1	High blood pressure	10.4
2	Smoking	7.1
3	High blood sugar	6.5
4	Air pollution (outdoor & indoor)	4.9
5	Obesity	4.7
6	Alcohol use	2.8
7	Diet low in fruits	2.4
8	Diet low in vegetables	1.5
9	Low physical activity	1.3
10	Unsafe water source	1.2

Source: Brookings
Published: June 2018

October 15

India's reduction of extreme poverty

No country wants to be named the place with the most people living in extreme poverty (less than $1.90 per day).

After decades in the top spot, India was recently eclipsed by Nigeria.

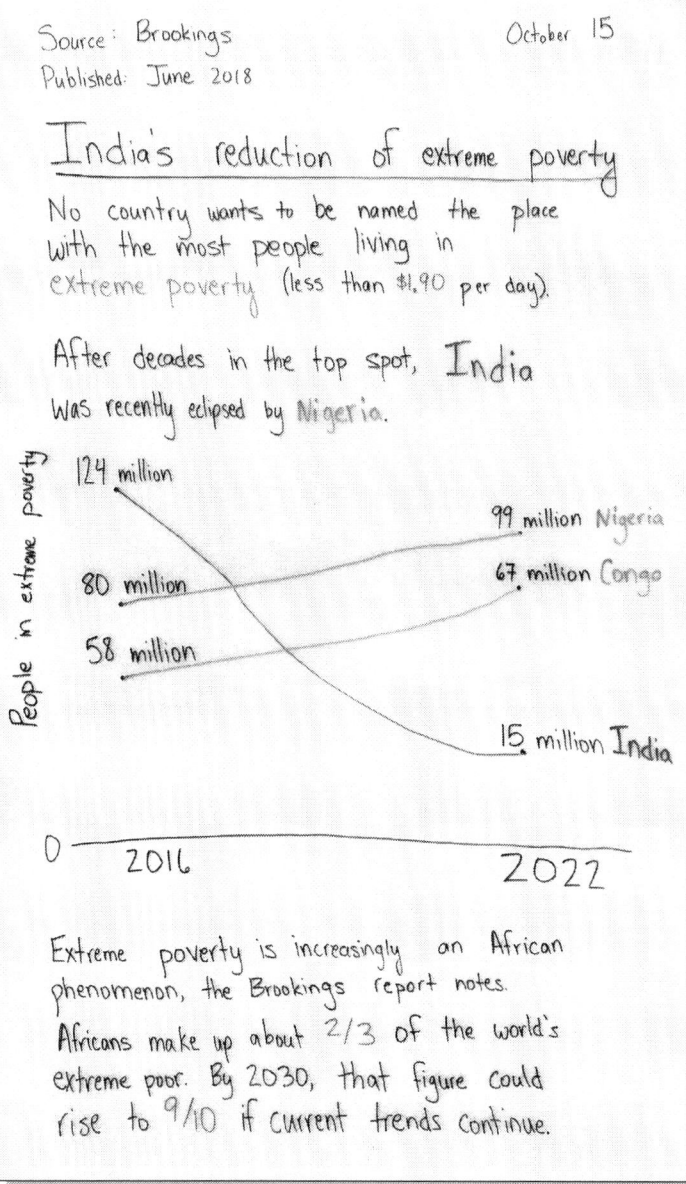

People in extreme poverty

124 million

99 million Nigeria

80 million

67 million Congo

58 million

15 million India

0 ——— 2016 ——— 2022

Extreme poverty is increasingly an African phenomenon, the Brookings report notes. Africans make up about 2/3 of the world's extreme poor. By 2030, that figure could rise to 9/10 if current trends continue.

Source: Brookings
Published: June 2018

India's Reduction of Extreme Poverty

No country wants to be named the place with the most people living in extreme poverty (less than $1.90 per day). After decades in the top spot, India was recently eclipsed by Nigeria.

Extreme poverty is increasingly an African phenomenon, the Brookings report noted. Africans make up about two-thirds of the world's extreme poor. By 2030, that figure could rise to nine-tenths if current trends continue.

Year	Country	Citizens million
2016	India	124
2016	Nigeria	80
2016	Congo	58
2022	India	15
2022	Nigeria	99
2022	Congo	67

Source: MIT Tech Review
Published: March 2019

Sanitation without sewers

2.3 billion people do not have basic sanitation facilities such as toilets or latrines

750 million people consume food irrigated by wastewater

842 K people die in low and middle income countries each year as a result of inadequate water sanitation and hygiene

892 million people defecate in the open, for example in street gutters, behind bushes, or into open bodies of water

Source: MIT Tech Review
Published: March 2019

Sanitation Without Sewers

- 2.3 billion people do not have basic sanitation facilities such as toilets or latrines.
- 750 million people consume food irrigated by wastewater.
- 842,000 people die in low and middle income countries each year as a result of inadequate water sanitation and hygiene.
- 892 million people defecate in the open, for example in street gutters, behind bushes, or into open bodies of water.

Source: GatesNotes
Published: Feb 2019

February 28

Africa is the yougst continent

While the rest of the world keeps getting older, the median age of Africa stays young. If they're healthy and educated, they will drive economic growth and innovation.

Kids aged 0-4

The rest of the world

Sub-Saharan Africa

600M 506M
500M
400M
300M
200M 173M
100M

357M
293M

2020   2100

Source: GatesNotes
Published: February 2019

Africa is the Youngest Continent

While the rest of the world keeps getting older, the median age of Africa — and especially sub-Saharan Africa — stays young. If they're healthy and educated, they will drive economic growth and innovation.

Median age in North America is *35 years old* while in Africa it is *18 years old*. For Kids 0–4, the rest of the world is shrinking while Africa is growing.

Source: UCLA

Published: November 2013

John Snow and the Broad Street Pump

Cholera is a bacterial disease causing severe diarrhea and dehydration. Between 1831 and 1854, tens of thousands of people in England died of cholera. At that time, the way cholera spread was a mystery, generally attributed to bad air.

In 1854 Soho, a suburb of London, was hit hard by an outbreak of cholera. Dr. John Snow who specialized in pregnancy and childbirth believed water or food was the true cause of the outbreak. To prove his hypothesis, he plotted cases of cholera on a map of Soho and identified a water pump in Broad Street as the source of the disease.

Dr. Snow had the pump handle removed, and cases of cholera immediately began to diminish. Researchers later discovered that this public well had been dug 3 feet from an old cesspit, which had begun to leak fecal bacteria.

This is a powerful application of data to save lives.

Source: UCLA
Published: November 2013

John Snow and the Broad Street Pump

Cholera is a bacterial disease causing severe diarrhea and dehydration. Between 1831 and 1854, tens of thousands of people in England died of cholera. At the time, the way that cholera spread was a mystery, generally attributed to bad air.

In 1854 Soho, a suburb of London, was hit hard by an outbreak of cholera. Dr. John Snow who specialized in pregnancy and childbirth believed water or food was the true cause of the outbreak. To prove his hypothesis, he plotted cases of cholera on a map of Soho and was able to identify a water pump in Broad Street as the source of the disease.

Dr. Snow had the pump handle removed, and cases of cholera immediately began to diminish. Researchers later discovered that this public well had been dug 3 feet from an old cesspit, which had begun to leak fecal bacteria.

This is a powerful application of data used to save lives.

The happiest countries in the world

The first World Happiness Report was published in April, 2012, in support of a UN meeting on happiness and well-being. The rankings of national happiness are based on a survey where respondents from 156 countries are asked to rate their own lives from 0 (the worst possible life) to 10 (the best possible life).

1. Finland
2. Denmark
3. Norway
4. Iceland
5. Netherlands
6. Switzerland
7. Sweden
8. New Zealand
9. Canada
10. Austria
11. Australia
12. Israel
13. Luxemburg
14. United Kingdom
15. Ireland
16. Germany
17. Belgium
18. United States

Source: 7th World Happiness Report
Published: March 2019

The Happiest Countries in the World

The first World Happiness Report was published in April 2012, in support of a UN meeting on happiness and well-being. The rankings of national happiness are based on a survey where respondents from *156 countries* are asked to rate their own lives from 0 (the worst possible life) to 10 (best possible life).

1. Finland
2. Denmark
3. Norway
4. Iceland
5. Netherlands
6. Switzerland
7. Sweden
8. New Zealand
9. Canada
10. Austria
11. Australia
12. Israel
13. Luxembourg
14. United Kingdom
15. Ireland
16. Germany
17. Belgium
18. United States

Source: The Economist   February 18, 2020
Published: January 2020

The Big Mac index

The Big Mac index compares the average McDonald's Big Mac hamburger price between countries. It is based on the theory of purchasing-power parity, the notion that in the long run exchange rates should move towards the rate that would equalize the price of a good in any two countries.

Most expensive		Least expensive	
Switzerland	$6.71	South Africa	$2.15
Norway	$5.97	Russia	$2.20
United States	$5.67	Romania	$2.21
Sweden	$5.44	Turkey	$2.21
Canada	$5.18	Malaysia	$2.33
Israel	$4.91	Azerbaijan	$2.33

Burgernomics seeks to make exchange-rate theory a bit more digestible.

Source: The Economist
Published: January 2020

The Big Mac Index

The Big Mac index compares the average *McDonald's Big Mac hamburger* price between countries. It is based on the theory of purchasing-power parity, the notion that in the long run exchange rates should move towards the rate that would equalize the price of a good in any two countries.

Most expensive:

- *Switzerland $6.71*
- *Norway $5.97*
- *United States $5.67*
- *Sweden $5.44*
- *Canada $5.18*
- *Israel $4.91*

Least expensive:

- *South Africa $2.15*
- *Russia $2.20*
- *Romania $2.21*
- *Turkey $2.21*
- *Malaysia $2.33*
- *Azerbaijan $2.33*

Burgernomics seeks to make exchange-rate theory a bit more *digestible.*

Source: Our World in Data

Published: September 2018

August 6

Literate and illiterate world population

Literacy rate of growth climbed in the middle of the 20th century, when the expansion of basic education became a global priority. The population for the estimate is 15 years and older.

Year	literate world population	illiterate world population
1820	12%	88
1880	20	80
1900	21	79
1920	32	68
1940	42	58
1960	61	39
1980	70	30
2000	82	18
2015	86	14

Source: Our World in Data
Published: September 2018

Literate and Illiterate World Population

Literacy rate of growth climbed in the middle of the 20th century, when the expansion of basic education became a global priority. The population for the estimate is 15 years and older.

Year	Literate World Population	Illiterate World Population
1820	12%	88%
1880	20%	80%
1900	21%	79%
1920	32%	68%
1940	42%	58%
1960	61%	39%
1980	70%	30%
2000	82%	18%
2015	86%	14%

Source: Harvard Business Review

Published: January 2020

A historical anecdote of good judgement

Good judgement is an interpretation of evidence that points to the right choice. People with good judgement are skeptical of information that doesn't make sense.

In 1983 Soviet lieutenant colonel Stanislav Petrov was advised that satellites had detected a U.S. missile attack on the Soviet Union. Petrov decided that the 100% probability reading was implausibly high and did not report the information upward, as were his instructions. Instead, he reported a system malfunction.

"I had all the data [to suggest a military attack was ongoing]. If I had sent my report up the chain of command, nobody would have said a word against it," said Petrov in 2013.

It turned out that the satellites had mistaken sunlight reflected from clouds for missile engines. In this moment, Stanislav Petrov used good judgement.

Source: Harvard Business Review
Published: January 2020

A Historical Anecdote of Good Judgement

Good judgment is an interpretation of evidence that points to the right choice. People with good judgment are skeptical of information that doesn't make sense.

In 1983 Soviet lieutenant colonel Stanislav Petrov was advised that satellites had detected a U.S. missile attack on the Soviet Union. Petrov decided that the *100%* probability reading was implausibly high and did not report the information upward, as were his instructions. Instead, he reported a system malfunction.

"I had all the data [to suggest a missile attack was ongoing]. If I had sent my report up the chain of command, nobody would have said a word against it," said Petrov in 2013.

It turned out that the satellites had mistaken sunlight reflected from clouds for missile engines. In this moment, Stanislav Petrov used good judgement.

Source: OAG Aviation
Published: March 2020

Global scheduled aviation capacity

OAG Aviation has been tracking the effect of the COVID-19 pandemic on aviation capacity since the start of the year.

The following chart shows the number of flights departing from various countries compared to the equivalent week in 2019.

Region	Monday, March 16, 2020 versus Monday, March 18, 2019
ALL	-12.4%
Hong Kong	-80.8
Italy	-73.9
South Korea	-56.1
China	-38.7
Singapore	-35.5
Germany	-30.2
UK	-19.3
Japan	-19.1
France	-13.7
Netherlands	-8.6
Australia	-2.9
USA	-0.5

Source: OAG Aviation
Published: March 2020

Global scheduled aviation capacity

OAG Aviation has been tracking the effect of the COVID-19 epidemic on aviation capacity since the start of the year.

The following chart shows the number of flights departing from various countries compared to the equivalent week in 2019.

Region	Monday March 16, 2020 versus Monday March 18, 2019
ALL	-12.4%
Hong Kong	-80.8%
Italy	-73.9%
South Korea	-56.1%
China	-38.7%
Singapore	-35.5%
Germany	-30.2%
UK	-19.3%
Japan	-19.1%
France	-13.7%
Netherlands	-8.6%
Australia	-2.9%
USA	-0.5%

Source: National Human Genome
Research Institute

Published: August 2020

October 23, 2020

DNA Sequencing Costs

"Genome sequencing is the equivalent of running spellcheck on every volume in a library," said Doctor David Miller.

Your genome includes all your DNA and contains important clues about you — from your ancestry to disease susceptibility, aging, and your body's response to medication.

The human genome was first sequenced in 2003 during a $3 billion, 13-year project, called The Human Genome Project.

Advances in genomics have led to substantial reductions in the cost of genome sequencing. Today, you can now get whole-genome sequencing for $599 from Nebula Genomics, an Amazon Launchpad member.

Compared to $3,000,000,000 17 years ago!

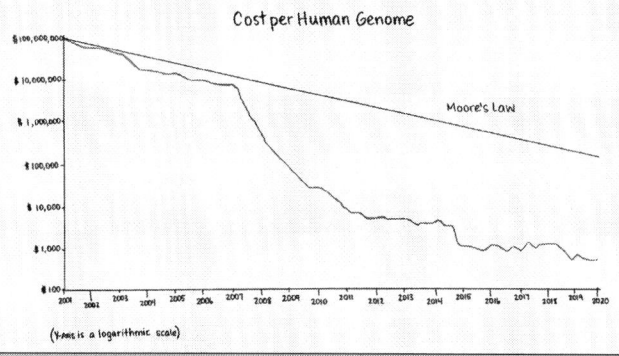

Cost per Human Genome

Moore's Law

(Y-axis is a logarithmic scale)

Source: National Human Genome Research Institute
Published: August 2020

DNA Sequencing Costs

"Genome sequencing is the equivalent of running spell check on every volume in a library," said Doctor David Miller.

Your genome includes all your DNA and contains important clues about you—from your ancestry to disease susceptibility, aging, and your body's response to medication.

The human genome was first sequenced in 2003 during a $3 billion, 13-year project.

Advances in genomics have led to substantial reductions in the cost of genome sequencing. Today, you can now get whole-genome sequencing for $599 from Nebula Genomics, an Amazon Launchpad member.

CHAPTER 19

GENERATIONAL TRENDS

Source: Cybba   March 28
Published: Jan. 2019

Who is Gen Z + why do they matter?

Who are they?
  Born mid-1990s to early 2000s.
  Not to be confused with Millenials.

Where did they come from?
  Gen Xers and Early Millenial parents.
  Don't want to go into any more detail than that :)

How big are they?
  24.7% of the US population

Do they spend?
  40% of all consumers in the next decade.

How are they different?
  85% research products before purchasing.

Screen of preference?
  Smartphone, median age for their
  first phone is 12 years old.

How many screens?

  5 on average, up from 3 for Millenials.

Source: Cybba
Published: January 2019

Who is Generation Z and Why Do They Matter?

Who are they? Born mid-1990s to early 2000s. Not to be confused with Millennials.

Where did they come from? Gen X'ers and Early Millennial parents.

How big are they? 24.7% of the US population

Do they spend? 40% of all consumers in the next decade.

How are they different? 85% research products before purchasing.

Screen of preference? Smartphone, median age for their first phone is 12 years old.

How many screens? 5 on average, up from 3 for Millennials.

Source: University of Michigan, Transportation Research
Published: August 2017

May 2

Younger generations are waiting longer to buy cars

Generation	% Buying Used Cars
Boomer	41%
Gen X	47
Gen Y	51
Gen Z	63

Share of Licensed Drivers by age

Age	1983	2017
19	84%	70%
18	81	61
17	69	44
16	45	23

Source: UMich Transportation Research Institute
Published: August 2017

Younger Generations are Waiting Longer to Buy Cars

Share of drivers buying used cars by generation:

Boomer — 41%

Gen X — 47%

Gen Y — 51%

Gen Z — 63%

Share of licensed drivers by age:

Age	1983	2017
19	84%	70%
18	81%	61%
17	69%	44%
16	45%	23%

Source: Piper Jaffray

Published: October 2019

n= 9,500 U.S. teens

February 10, 2020

U.S. teen preferences

The investment bank Piper Jaffray surveys teens twice a year to keep up with their fast-changing preferences. With students from 42 states and an average age of 15.8 years old, here are Gen Z's results.

Daily video consumption

YouTube	37%
Netfix	35
Cable	12
Hulu	7
Prime Video	3

Top restaurants

Chick-fil-A	18%
Starbucks	11
Chipotle	6
McDonald's	5
Dunkin Donuts	4

Top shopping websites

Amazon	52%
Nike	4
American Eagle	3
Urban Outfitters	2
eBay	2

Top footwear brands

Nike	42%
Vans	20
adidas	13
Converse	4
Foot Locker	3

Source: Piper Jaffray
Published: October 2019
n= 9,500 U.S. teens

U.S. Teen Preferences

The investment bank Piper Jaffray surveys teens twice a year to keep up with their fast-changing preferences. With students from 42 states with an average age of 15.8 years old, here are Gen Z's results:

Top Footwear Brands	Respondents	Top Restaurants	Respondents
Nike	42%	Chick-fil-A	18%
Vans	20%	Starbucks	11%
adidas	13%	Chipotle	6%
Converse	4%	McDonald's	5%
Foot Locker	3%	Dunkin Donuts	4%

Top Shopping Websites	Respondents	Daily Video Consumption	Respondents
Amazon	52%	YouTube	37%
Nike	4%	Netflix	35%
American Eagle	3%	Cable	12%
Urban Outfitters	2%	Hulu	7%
eBay	2%	Prime Video	3%

Source: Expedia
Published: January 2018
n= 1,254 U.S. adults

March 4, 2020

Travel trends among generations

- The long weekend (3-5 days) is the most preferred length of time for a leisure trip for Millennials, Gen X, and Gen Z. Baby Boomers are much more likely to travel a week or longer.

- 81% of Gen Z travelers feel obligated to send texts to family or a significant other before takeoff and after landing.

- 57% of Americans are currently saving money for travel. Millennials are the highest age group at 65%.

- 36% of Gen Z travelers have chosen a destination specifically because they saw postings about the destination on social media.

- 27% of Millennials have posted a potential trip on social media to canvas opinions before booking.

Definitions:
Baby Boomers 1946 to 1964   Millennials 1977 to 1995
Gen X 1965 to 1976   Gen Z 1996 and after
(survey age 18+)

Source: Expedia
Published: January 2018
n = 1,254 U.S. adults

Travel Trends Among Generations

- The long weekend (3-5 days) is the most preferred length of time for a leisure trip for Millennials, Gen X, and Gen Z. Baby Boomers are much more likely to travel for a week or longer.
- 81% of Gen Z travelers feel obligated to send texts to family or a significant other before takeoff and after landing.
- 57% of Americans are currently saving money for travel. Millennials are the highest age group at 65%.
- 36% of Gen Z travelers have chosen a destination specifically because they saw postings about the destination on social media.
- 27% of Millennials have posted a potential trip on social media to canvas opinions before booking!

Baby Boomers are defined in this report as born between 1946 and 1964, Gen X from 1965 to 1976, Millennials from 1977 to 1995, and Gen Z from 1996 and after (survey age 18+).

Source: Zebra IQ
Published: September 2020

October 5, 2020

Gen Z Trends

Who is Gen Z?

- Born between 1995 and 2010
- 3 billion of them worldwide
- 35% of the global population
- The mobile-first generation

What can we learn about them?

- 62% of their political news comes from social media
- 90% support Black Lives Matter (a 17-year old built the most widely spread page of resources)
- 21% feel they spend too much time on TikTok
- 35% feel like their mental health has worsened during the COVID-19 pandemic

Source: Zebra IQ
Published: September 2020

Gen Z Trends

Who is Gen Z?

- Born between 1995 and 2010
- 3 billion of them worldwide
- 35% of the global population
- The mobile-first generation

What can we learn about them?

- 62% of their political news comes from social media
- 90% support Black Lives Matter (a 17-year old built the most widely spread page of resources)
- 21% feel they spend too much time on TikTok
- 35% feel like their mental health has worsened during the COVID-19 pandemic

Source: Charles Schwab   December 31

Published: December 2019

n = 142,000 retirement plan participants

Equity holdings by generation

To understand how investment varies by generation, Charles Schwab looked at the top ten equities within retirement accounts.

	Millenials Age 27-38	Gen X Age 39-54	Baby Boomers Age 55-72
1	Amazon	Apple	Apple
2	Apple	Amazon	Amazon
3	Tesla	Berkshire Hathaway	Berkshire Hathaway
4	Facebook	Facebook	Microsoft
5	Grayscale Bitcoin Trust	Microsoft	Facebook
6	Berkshire Hathaway	Tesla	Visa
7	Disney	Alphabet (Google)	Alphabet (Google)
8	Netflix	Netflix	AT&T
9	Microsoft	Alibaba	Boeing
10	Alibaba	Visa	Alibaba

Source: Charles Schwab
Published: December 2019
n = 142,000 retirement plan participants

Equity Holdings by Generation

To understand how investment decisions varied by generation, Charles Schwab looked at the top ten equities within retirement accounts.

Millennials (Age 27-38)		Gen X (Age 39-54)		Baby Boomers (Age 55-72)	
AMAZON	7.9%	APPLE	10.5%	APPLE	9.2%
APPLE	6.2%	AMAZON	7.2%	AMAZON	5.3%
TESLA	3.2%	BERKSHIRE HATHAWAY	2.4%	BERKSHIRE HATHAWAY	2.8%
FACEBOOK	3.0%	FACEBOOK	2.3%	MICROSOFT	2.7%
GRAYSCALE BITCOIN TRUST	1.8%	MICROSOFT	2.2%	FACEBOOK	1.4%
BERKSHIRE HATHAWAY	1.7%	TESLA	1.5%	VISA	1.3%
DISNEY	1.7%	ALPHABET (GOOGLE)	1.3%	ALPHABET (GOOGLE)	1.2%
NETFLIX	1.6%	NETFLIX	1.3%	AT&T	1.2%
MICROSOFT	1.5%	ALIBABA	1.2%	BOEING	1.1%
ALIBABA	1.4%	VISA	1.2%	ALIBABA	1.0%

Source: American Institute of CPAs   February 11, 2020
Published: March 2019
n=631 Certified Public Accountant (CPA) financial planners

Retirement anxiety

A survey of CPA financial planners explored what factors are impacting clients' retirement planning peace of mind. Clients' top three financial concerns for retirement are:

Top Financial Concern	2018	2016
1) Running out of money	30%	41%
2) Maintaining current lifestyle	28	29
3) Rising healthcare costs	18	11

Most frequently listed among the top three sources of client concern for outliving their money:

Concern	Respondents who listed among top three concerns
1) Healthcare costs	77%
2) Market fluctuations	53
3) Unexpected costs	50
4) Lifestyle expenses	42
5) The possibility of being a financial burden on their relatives	22

Source: American Institute of CPAs
Published: March 2019
n = 631 Certified Public Accountant financial planners

Retirement Anxiety

A survey of CPA financial planners explored what factors are impacting clients' retirement planning peace of mind.

Clients' top three financial concerns for retirement are:

	Top Financial Concern	2018	2016
1	Running out of money	30%	41%
2	Maintaining current lifestyle	28%	29%
3	Rising healthcare costs	18%	11%

Most frequently listed as the top three sources of client concern for outliving their money:

	Concern	Respondents who listed among top three concerns
1	Healthcare costs	77%
2	Market fluctuations	53%
3	Unexpected costs	50%
4	Lifestyle expenses	42%
5	The possibility of being a financial burden on their relatives	22%

Source: How Machines are Affecting
People and Places
Published: January 2019

Which jobs are at risk?

Researchers predict that routine physical
and cognitive tasks will be the
most susceptible to automation.
The chart below is the automation
potential by major occupation group.

Occupation	Annual Salary (average)	Automation potential
Food service	$23,900	81%
Production	37,200	79
Administration	37,300	60
Agriculture	27,800	56
Transportation	36,100	55
Construction	48,900	50
Maintenance	46,700	49
Sales	40,600	43
Legal	106,000	38

Source: How Machines are Affecting People and Places
Published: January 2019

Which Jobs are at Risk?

Researchers predict that routine physical and cognitive tasks will be the most susceptible to automation. The chart below is the automation potential by major occupation group.

Occupation	Average Annual Salary	Automation Potential
Food service	$23,900	81%
Production	$37,200	79%
Administrative	$37,300	79%
Agriculture	$27,800	56%
Transportation	$36,100	55%
Construction	$48,900	50%
Maintenance	$46,700	49%
Sales	$40,600	43%
Legal	$106,000	38%

Source: JAMA Internal Medicine   March 5, 2020
Published: February 2020
n = 14,000 U.S. adults

Cannabis use among older adults

The percentage of U.S. adults over the age of 65 who used some form of cannabis in the past year was 75% higher in 2018 than 2015 (4.2% and 2.4%). In 2006, just 0.4% of people in the 65+ age group reported using cannabis. The rise was highest among racial and ethical minorities +336%, those previously treated for mental health issues +157%, and women +93%.

"Ten years ago, no one asked me about cannabis use ever. Now, it's a very common question when I'm in the clinic. There's a lot of interest."

- Dr. Benjamin Han of the New York University School of Medicine (study author and genriatrician)

Source: JAMA Internal Medicine
Published: February 2020
n = 14,000 U.S. adults

Cannabis Use Among Older Adults

The percentage of U.S. adults over the age of 65 who used some form of cannabis in the past year was 75% higher in 2018 than 2015 (4.2% and 2.4%). In 2006, just 0.4% of people 65+ reported using cannabis. The rise was highest among racial and ethnic minorities (+336%), those previously treated for mental health issues (+157%), and women (+93%).

"Ten years ago, no one asked me about cannabis use ever. Now, it's a very common question when I'm in the clinic. There's a lot of interest."

—**Dr. Benjamin Han of the New York University School of Medicine (study author and geriatrician)**

Source: Stanford, Department of Sociology
Published: July 2019
n = 5,421 heterosexual couples

The internet has changed how couples meet

For heterosexual couples in the U.S, meeting online has become the most popular way couples meet, eclipsing meeting through friends and family for the first time around 2013. The researchers find that internet meeting is displacing the roles that family and friends once played in bringing couples together.

How couples met*	1995	2017	Change
online	2%	39%	+37%
through friends	33	20	-13
through family	15	7	-8
through or as coworkers	19	11	-8
in a bar/restaurant	19	27	+8
in a primary or secondary school	10	5	-5
in church	7	4	-3
through or as neighbors	8	3	-5
in college	9	4	-5

*can be more than 1, such as meeting at a bar in college.

Source: Stanford, Department of Sociology
Published: July 2019
n = 5,421 heterosexual couples

The Internet Has Changed How Couples Meet

For heterosexual couples in the U.S., meeting online has become the most popular way couples meet, eclipsing meeting through friends for the first time around 2013. The researchers find that Internet meeting is displacing the roles that family and friends once played in bringing couples together.

How Couples Met*	1995	2017	Change
Online	2%	39%	37%
Through friends	33%	20%	-13%
Through family	15%	7%	-8%
Through or as coworkers	19%	11%	-8%
In a bar/Restaurant	19%	27%	8%
In a primary or secondary school	10%	5%	-5%
In church	7%	4%	-3%
Through or as neighbors	8%	3%	-5%
In college	9%	4%	-5%

*Can be more than 1, such as meeting at a bar in college.

Source: Stanford and Benedict Evans   February 14, 2020
Published: January 2020

The growth of online dating

Stanford sociologist Michael Rosenfeld found that heterosexual couples are more likely to meet a romantic partner online than through personal contacts and connections. Since 1940, traditional ways of meeting partners - through family, in church, and in the neighborhood — have all been in decline. This study did not include homosexual couples.

U.S. heterosexual couples who met online

Source: Stanford and Benedict Evans
Published: January 2020

The Growth of Online Dating

Stanford sociologist Michael Rosenfeld found that heterosexual couples are more likely to meet a romantic partner online than through personal contacts and connections. Since 1940, traditional ways of meeting partners — through family, in church and in the neighborhood — have all been in decline. This study did not include homosexual couples.

39% of heterosexual couples reported meeting their partner online, compared to 22% in 2009.

CHAPTER 20

CLIMATE CRISIS

Source: Our World in Data
Published: January 2020
n= 38,000 farms in 119 countries

March 23, 2020

Greenhouse gas emissions by food

There are massive differences in the greenhouse gas emissions (CO_2-equivalents) of different foods.
The table below shows the kilograms of greenhouse gas emissions per one kilogram of food product produced.
For example, producing 1 kg of beef emits 59.6 kilograms of greenhouse gases.

Food product	Land use change (e.g., deforestation)	Animal Feed and farm	Processing, transportation, packaging, and retail	Total
Beef	16.3	41.3	2.0	59.6
Cheese	4.5	15.4	1.3	21.2
Dark chocolate	14.3	3.7	0.7	18.7
Coffee	3.7	10.4	2.4	16.5
Shrimps (farmed)	0.2	10.9	0.7	11.8
Poultry meat	2.5	2.5	1.1	6.1
Eggs	0.7	3.5	0.3	4.5
Tofu	1.0	0.5	1.5	3.0
Milk	0.5	1.7	0.6	2.8
Wine	-0.1	0.6	0.9	1.4
Bananas	0.0	0.3	0.5	0.8
Potatoes	0.0	0.2	0.1	0.3
Nuts	-2.1	2.1	0.2	0.2

Source: Our World in Data
Published: January 2020
n = 38,000 farms in 119 countries

Greenhouse Gas Emissions By Food

There are massive differences in the greenhouse gas emissions (CO2-equivalents) of different foods. The chart below shows the kilograms of greenhouse gas emissions per one kilogram of food product produced. For example, producing *1 kilogram* of beef emits *59.6 kilograms* of greenhouse gases.

Food product	Land use change (e.g., deforestation)	Animal feed and farm	Processing, transportation, packaging, and retail	Total
Beef	16.3	41.3	2.0	59.6
Cheese	4.5	15.4	1.3	21.2
Dark Chocolate	14.3	3.7	0.7	18.7
Coffee	3.7	10.4	2.4	16.5
Shrimps (farmed)	0.2	10.9	0.7	11.8
Poultry Meat	2.5	2.5	1.1	6.1
Eggs	0.7	3.5	0.3	4.5
Tofu	1.0	0.5	1.5	3.0
Milk	0.5	1.7	0.6	2.8
Wine	-0.1	0.6	0.9	1.4
Bananas	0.0	0.3	0.5	0.8
Potatoes	0.0	0.2	0.1	0.3
Nuts	-2.1	2.1	0.2	0.2

Source: Center for Sustainable Systems, UMich
Published: November 2018

May 9

The Carbon footprint of meal kits

$8.1 \text{ kg } CO_2/\text{meal} \rightarrow$ grocery meal ⎫
$6.1 \text{ kg } CO_2/\text{meal} \rightarrow$ meal kits ⎬ greenhouse gas emissions are 33% higher for grocery meals compared to meal kits.

Drivers of the difference

- Streamlined and direct-to-consumer supply chains ($-1.05 \text{ kg } CO_2/\text{meal}$)

- Reduced food waste (-0.86)

- Lower last-mile transportation emissions (-0.45)

- Refrigeration packs compared to retail refrigeration (-0.37)

- Increases in food packaging ($+0.17$)

Meal Kit examples:
- Amazon Meal Kits
- Blue Apron
- Plated
- HelloFresh
- Home Chef
- Terra's Kitchen

Source: Center for Sustainable Systems, UMich
Published: November 2018

The Carbon Footprint of Meal Kits Compared with Grocery Meals

On average, grocery meal greenhouse gas emissions are *33%* higher than meal kits (8.1 kg CO_2e/grocery meal versus 6.1 kg CO_2e/meal kit meal)

Drivers of the Difference

Driver	Meal kit meal relative to grocery meal (in kg CO2e/meal)
Streamlined and direct-to-consumer supply chains	−1.05
Reduced food waste	−0.86
Lower last-mile transportation emissions	−0.45
Refrigeration packs compared with retail refrigeration	−0.37
Increases in food packaging	0.17

Meal Kit examples:
- Amazon Meal Kits
- Blue Apron
- Plated
- HelloFresh
- Home Chef
- Terra's Kitchen

Source: Our World in Data
Published: October 2019

CO_2 emissions per capita

In this chart, we see the countries that generate the most CO_2 per capita in 2017. The global average in 2017 was 4.8 tons per person.

Rank	Country	CO_2 emissions per capita (tons)
1	Qatar	49
2	Trinidad and Tobago	30
3	Kuwait	25
4	United Arab Emirates	25
5	Brunei	24
6	Bahrain	23
7	Saudi Arabia	19
8	Australia	17
9	United States	16
10	Kazakhstan	16
11	Luxembourg	16
12	Canada	16
13	Estonia	15
14	Palau	14
15	Oman	14

Source: Our World in Data
Published: October 2019

CO₂ Emissions Per Capita

In this chart, we see the countries that generated the most CO_2 per capita in 2017. The global average in 2017 was *4.8 tons* per person.

Rank	Country	CO2 emissions per capita (tons)
1	Qatar	49
2	Trinidad and Tobago	30
3	Kuwait	25
4	United Arab Emirates	25
5	Brunei	24
6	Bahrain	23
7	Saudi Arabia	19
8	Australia	17
9	United States	16
10	Kazakhstan	16
11	Luxembourg	16
12	Canada	16
13	Estonia	15
14	Palau	14
15	Oman	14

Source: IPCC
Published: 2014

As seen in: Bill + Melinda Gates' Annual Letter

February 26

Greenhouse gas emissions, by sector

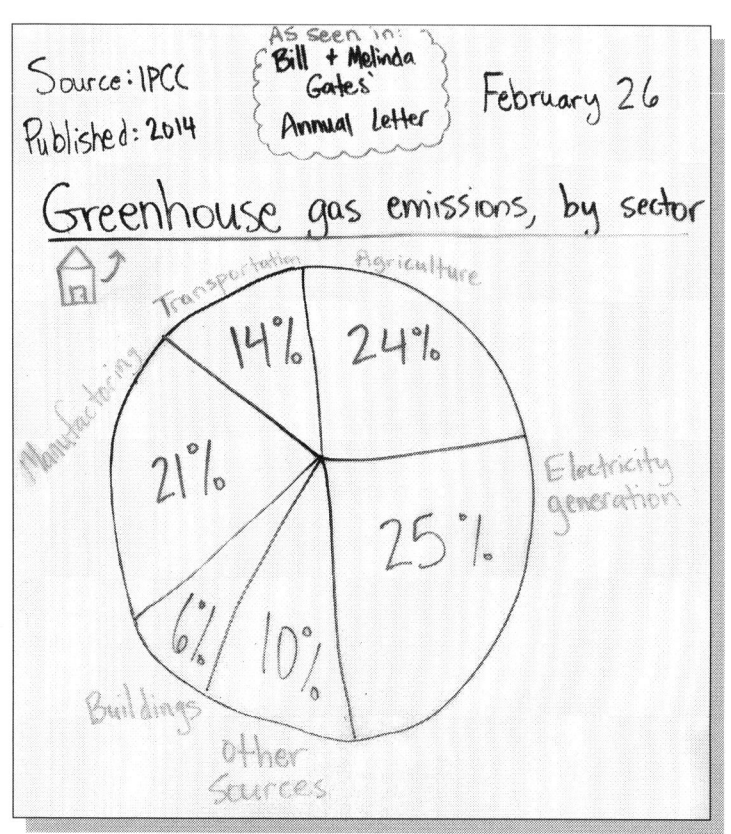

Source: IPCC
Published: 2014

Greenhouse Gas Emissions, by Sector

Sector	% of greenhouse gas emissions
Electricity generation	25
Agriculture	24
Transportation	14
Manufacturing	21
Buildings	6
Other sources	10

As seen in the Bill and Melinda Gates Annual Letter.

Source: International Energy Agency
Published: 2014

August 9

Carbon dioxide emissions by sector

Carbon dioxide (CO_2) is known as a greenhouse gas that absorbs and emits thermal radiation, creating the 'greenhouse effect'.

Sector	1960	2014	Change in basis points
Manufacturing industries and construction	29.3%	20.0	-934 bps
Electricity and heat production	28.6	49.0	+2048
Residential buildings, commercial, and public services	20.4	8.6	-1175
Transport	19.2	20.5	+128
Other sectors	2.5	1.9	-65
TOTAL	100.0	100.0	

Source: International Energy Agency
Published: 2014

Carbon Dioxide (CO₂) Emissions by Sector or Source, World

Carbon dioxide (CO2) is known as a greenhouse gas — a gas that absorbs and emits thermal radiation, creating the *'greenhouse effect'*.

Sector	1960	2014	Change (basis points)
Manufacturing industries and construction	29.3%	20.0%	-934
Electricity and heat production	28.6%	49.0%	2048
Residential buildings & commercial and public services	20.4%	8.6%	-1175
Transport	19.2%	20.5%	128
Other sectors	2.5%	1.9%	-65
TOTAL	**100.0%**	**100.0%**	

Source: World Economic Forum

Published: January 2016

December 4

The Industrial Revolutions

The First Industrial Revolution used water and steam power to mechanize production.

The Second used electrical power and internal combustion engines to create mass production.

The Third used electronics and information technology to automate mass production.

The Fourth uses hardware, software, and biology to create cyber-physical systems. When billions of people connect via mobile devices, emerging technologies include:

- Robotics
- Artificial Intelligence
- Nanotechnology
- Quantum computing
- Biotechnology
- The Internet of Things
- Decentralized Concensus
- 5G
- 3D printing
- Fully autonomous vehicles
- Energy storage

Source: World Economic Forum
Published: January 2016

The Industrial Revolutions

The **First** Industrial Revolution used water and steam power to mechanize production.

The **Second** used electric power and internal combustion engines to create mass production.

The **Third** used electronics and information technology to automate mass production.

The **Fourth** uses hardware, software, and biology to create cyber-physical systems.

When billions of people connect via mobile devices, emerging technologies include:

- robotics
- artificial intelligence
- nanotechnology
- quantum computing
- biotechnology
- the internet of things
- decentralized consensus
- 5G
- 3D printing
- fully autonomous vehicles
- energy storage

Source: Bloomberg
Published: June 2020

Norway's carbon capture

Norway is on track to become the world's top destination for carbon capture infrastructure. Lawmakers will decide this year whether to contribute the majority of funds for a $2.6 billion project to bury carbon dioxide emissions under their seabed.

- In early trials, carbon dioxide emissions from a cement factory and a power plant would be compressed and buried beneath the seabed.

- At $140 per metric ton, the project would run five times the current price for diverting carbon dioxide emissions from the atmosphere.

- Norway's investment would pale in comparison to government subsidies currently provided to purchases of electric cars, an expenditure that amounts to $1,350 per ton of carbon dioxide suppressed.

Source: Bloomberg
Published: June 2020

Norway's Carbon Capture

Norway is on track to become the world's top destination for carbon capture infrastructure. Lawmakers will decide this year whether to contribute the majority of funds for a $2.6 billion project to bury carbon dioxide emissions under their seabed.

- In early trials, carbon dioxide emissions from a cement factory and a power plant would be compressed and buried beneath the seabed.
- At $140 per metric ton, the project would run five times the current price for diverting carbon dioxide emissions from the atmosphere.
- Norway's investment would pale in comparison to government subsidies currently provided to purchasers of electric cars, an expenditure that amounts to $1,350 per ton of carbon dioxide suppressed.

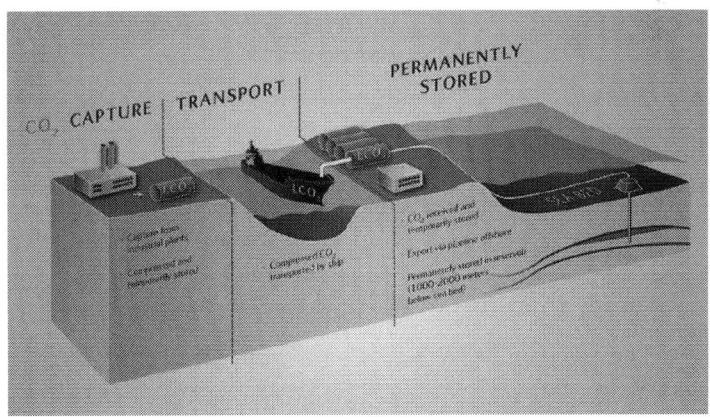

Illustration of the full chain of the Northern Lights
carbon capture project. Source: Equinor.

CHAPTER 21

SPACE

Source: Blue Origin
Published: February 2020

Blue Origin's Mission

Back in 1982, eighteen year old future Amazon founder Jeff Bezos told the Miami Herald that he one day wanted to build space hotels, amusement parks, and colonies for millions of people orbiting the earth.

In 2000, Bezos founded Blue Origin with the goal of achieving "millions of people living and working in space to benefit Earth." The company's three key programs include:

New Shepard: a reusable rocket capable of carrying astronauts and research payloads on 11 minute suborbital flights into space. Launched successfully in November 2015.

New Glenn: a reusable rocket that Blue Origin calls, "the vehicle that will build the road to space", capable of carrying passengers and heavy payloads into Earth's orbit and beyond, scheduled to launch in 2021.

Blue Moon: a versatile lander to deliver cargo and crew to the lunar surface, a major milestone in the company's mission to establish sustained human presence on the moon, first mission scheduled for 2024.

Source: Blue Origin
Published: February 2020

Blue Origin's Mission

Back in 1982, eighteen-year-old future Amazon founder Jeff Bezos told the Miami Herald that he one day wanted to build space hotels, amusement parks, and colonies for millions of people orbiting the earth.

In 2000, Bezos founded Blue Origin with the goal of achieving "millions of people living and working in space to benefit Earth." The company's three key programs include:

- **New Shepard:** a reusable rocket capable of carrying astronauts and research payloads on 11-minute sub-orbital flights into space. Launched successfully in November 2015.
- **New Glenn:** a reusable rocket that Blue Origin calls, "the vehicle that will build the road to space," capable of carrying passengers and heavy payloads into earth's orbit and beyond, scheduled to launch in 2021.
- **Blue Moon:** a versatile lander to deliver cargo and crew to the lunar surface, a major milestone in the company's mission to establish sustained human presence on the moon, first mission scheduled for 2024.

Source: Inverse
Published: April 2019

May 3

"We had 5 petabytes of data recorded"
    -Dan Marrone, Ph.D. @ the University of Arizona

The black hole at the center of
Messier 87 resides 55 million light-years
from Earth and has a mass 6.5 billion
times that of our sun.

Over seven days in April 2017,
telescopes in Chile, Hawaii, Arizona, Mexico, Spain, and South Pole
tilted toward M87. Synchronized by atomic clocks,
they all started collecting the incoming radio
signals and logging the data on
super-fast data recorders built
for this very task.

Source: Inverse
Published: April 2019

A black hole 55 million light-years away

The black hole at the center of Messier 87 resides 55 million light-years from Earth and has a mass 6.5 billion times that of our Sun.

Over seven days in April 2017, eight telescopes (Chile, Hawaii, Arizona, Mexico, Spain and at the South Pole) tilted toward M87. Synchronized by atomic clocks, they all started collecting the incoming radio signals and logging the data on super-fast data recorders that had been built for this very task.

"We had 5 petabytes of data recorded."

—Dan Marrone, Ph.D. at U of Arizona who specialized in data storage for the experiment.

Source: Berkeley
Published: May 2019

Using satellite images to bet on retailers

Using 4.8 million satellite images of parking lots from 2011 to 2017 covering 44 major U.S. retailers, including Walmart, Target, Costco, and Whole Foods Market, the researchers confirmed that year-over-year changes in the number of cars in individual stores' parking lots is a reliable predictor of quarterly sales.

The informational advantage yields 4 to 5% in the three days around quarterly earning calls.

This type of satellite data has been commercially available since 2011, but the information hasn't spread far beyond hedge funds.

Source: Berkeley
Published: May 2019

Using Satellite Images to Bet on Retailers

Using 4.8 million satellite images of parking lots from 2011 to 2017 covering 44 major U.S. retailers, including Walmart, Target, Costco, and Whole Foods Market, the researchers confirmed that year-over-year changes in the number of cars in individual stores' parking lots is a reliable predictor of quarterly sales.

The informational advantage yields 4% — 5% in the 3 days around quarterly earnings announcements.

This type of satellite data has been commercially available since 2011, but the information hasn't spread far beyond hedge funds.

Source: Space News   October 2, 2020

Published: February 2009

When Satellites Collide

More than 2,500 military and commercial satellites orbit the earth. In the rare instances when satellites collide, they create space debris capable of damaging other satellites or the International Space Station.

In February 2009, the satellites Iridium 33 and Kosmos-2251 collided at 42,000 km/h (26,000 mph).

In July 2016, a piece of space debris hit Maxar's WorldView-2.

Today, there are 34,000 debris objects over 10 centimeters (4 inches) orbiting the earth. Despite calls for the mandatory disposal of defunct satellites, there is no international agreement that exists.

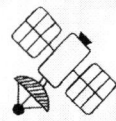

Source: Space News
Published: February 2009

When Satellites Collide

More than 2,500 military and commercial satellites orbit the earth. In the rare instances when satellites collide, they create space debris capable of damaging other satellites or the International Space Station.

In February 2009, the satellites Iridium 33 and Kosmos-2251 collided at 42,000 km/h (26,000 mph).

In July 2016, a piece of space debris hit Maxar's World-View-2.

Today, there are 34,000 debris objects over 10 centimeters (4 inches) orbiting the earth. Despite calls for the mandatory disposal of defunct satellites, there is no international agreement that exists.

Source: MIT Tech Review   April 30, 2020

Published: April 2020

Satellite mega-constellations

More than 3.5 billion people lack internet access. Companies like SpaceX and OneWeb think they can deliver broadband internet to the planet by launching mega-constellations of thousands of satellites.

The mega-constellations are feasible because we have learned to build smaller satellites and launch them more cheaply. During the space shuttle era (1972 to 2011), launching a satellite into space cost roughly $24,800 per pound. Today a SpaceX Falcon 9 launch costs about $1,240 per pound.

The upside: thousands of satellites could supply internet access for even the poorest and most remote populations on the planet.

The downside: a collision could cause millions of pieces of space debris, making satellite services and future space exploration next to impossible.

Source: MIT Tech Review
Published: April 2020

Satellite Mega-Constellations

More than 3.5 billion people lack internet access. Companies like SpaceX and OneWeb think they can deliver broadband internet to the planet by launching mega-constellations of thousands of satellites.

The mega-constellations are feasible because we have learned to build smaller satellites and launch them more cheaply. During the space shuttle era (1972-2011), launching a satellite into space cost roughly $24,800 per pound. Today a SpaceX Falcon 9 launch costs about $1,240 per pound.

The upside: thousands of satellites could supply internet access for even the poorest and most remote populations on the planet.

The downside: a collision could cause millions of pieces of space debris, making satellite services and future space exploration next to impossible.

CONGRATULATIONS!

You've reached the end of the book. Hungry for more facts? Sign up for the email newsletter at **www.factoftheday1.com.**

Made in the USA
Monee, IL
08 February 2021

34436035-17e7-4ac8-8c8c-813f986b90baR01